Coley
Happy Christmas 2010
XX
Clixen

Under the Spotlight

Under the Spotlight

Conversations with 17 Leading Irish Journalists

Roger Greene

The Liffey Press

Published by
The Liffey Press
Ashbrook House
10 Main Street, Raheny,
Dublin 5, Ireland
www.theliffeypress.com

A catalogue record of this book is
available from the British Library.

ISBN 1-904148-82-4

Printed in Spain by Graficas Cems.

$\mathcal{C}$ontents

About the Author

An arts graduate of Trinity College, Dublin, Roger Greene is a radio broadcaster, documentary filmmaker, journalist and Lecturer in Radio Broadcasting and Media with the Dun Laoghaire Institute of Art, Design and Technology. He presents a two-hour Sunday lunchtime radio show, *Media Matters*, on Dublin's Newstalk 106, from which the interviews in *Under the Spotlight* have been taken.

$\mathcal{A}$cknowledgements

If I've unwittingly omitted your name here, please accept my apologies and my thanks for your input and support.

First of all, *Media Matters* would not have functioned over the past three years without the following who supported, encouraged and contributed to the programme or helped with this book: Dan Healy; Damien Kiberd; Patrick Hand; Fiona Stack; Brian Regan; Eoin Dolan; Pete Lunn; Amanda Browne; Aidan Dunne; Tom Lawlor; Steve MacDonald; Justin Dawson; Conor Hogan; Sean Doyle, Olive Cummins, Kyla West and Emma Woods.

There have been a number of producers on *Media Matters* since its inception. They include: Jonathan Doyle, the first to produce *Media Matters* and who was instrumental in shaping the programme; Susan Cahill, an endearing whirlwind of energy and enthusiasm; John O'Donovan, who provides production cover, doubles as stand-in presenter and always brings an extra dimension to any programme; Brendan Howard, whose time on the programme was all too brief; and Paddy McDonnell, producer for the last 18 months who lives by the dictum, "Be reasonable, do it my way". Nevertheless, his thorough approach to producing ensures the programme happens every Sunday. Paddy lines up the guests on the programme, including the 17 journalists featured in this book.

A number of people have "sat in" for me in my absences including Declan Carty, Orla Barry, John O'Donovan, Emmet Oliver, Mary Minihan, David Murphy and Colm O'Mongain.

I thank the following for their support and help: Sean Larkin; Tony McGuinness; Faith O'Grady; Toni Delany; Michael McNally. A special word of thanks to Donald Taylor Black, friend, colleague and mentor since Trinity College days; and to Guy St John Williams, lifelong friend and seasoned author whose advice and encouragement on this and other projects over the years has been immense.

And of course my thanks to publishers The Liffey Press, specifically David Givens, Brian Langan and Heidi Murphy for their help, valuable advice and encouragement on the project. And to Sinéad McKenna for her excellent design work.

Photo credits: The author and publishers are grateful to the following photographers and organisations for permission to reproduce their photographs on the cover and in the chapters of this book: *The Irish Times* (Conor Brady, Lara Marlowe); Newstalk 106 (Eamon Dunphy, *Media Matters* team); McConnells PR (Carol Flynn); *Sunday Tribune* (Nóirín Hegarty); James Bareham and HarperCollins (Fergal Keane); *Sunday Independent* (Gene Kerrigan); *Sunday Times* (Damien Kiberd); David Conachy, *Sunday Independent* (Caroline Morahan); John Eagle (Denis Tuohy); John McIlroy (John Waters); and Liza Cauldwell (Roger Greene). These photographs remain the copyright of the named individuals and organisations. While every effort has been made to identify copyright holders, not all could be traced; we apologise for any omissions or errors.

For Mary, Cara and Anna

Introduction

A career in media is one of chance and change. Many media people are unsure quite how they've ended up where they are, as you will see from some of the journalists interviewed in this collection of radio conversations. I'm no different and the path that delivered me to Newstalk 106 when it first went to air in April 2002 is a curious one.

From 1998 to 2001 I was chief executive of the newly founded Screen Commission of Ireland. It was a three-year contract to establish and run Ireland's first film and television commission under the then Department of Arts, Heritage, Gaeltacht and the Islands, and the Irish Film Board. With a year to run on my contract, it became clear that the Screen Commission would be a short-lived entity. There wasn't room for two state-funded film agencies and the work of the Screen Commission would be subsumed into the already long established Irish Film Board.

What next?

Rumours were circulating that Newstalk 106, Ireland's first all-talk radio station, was about to start broadcasting. At that stage I had taken up my present position as a lecturer in media with the Department of Film and Media in the Institute of Art, Design and Technology, Dun Laoghaire. However, I wanted to keep my hand in production and duly approached Newstalk 106 about work as a freelance producer.

In 2002 I met with the station's start-up editor Pete Lunn, ex-BBC, where he had been deputy editor of *Newsnight*. At some point the conversation veered from producing to presenting and I found myself agreeing to do a couple of pilot programmes. I explained that whereas I had been a regular contributor to BBC local radio and to RTÉ Radio, I had never presented. This didn't seem to be a problem.

Having completed the pilot programmes, Newstalk offered me a two-hour Sunday lunchtime slot. The station would be going to air within a couple of weeks, as would I.

Jonathan Doyle, who joined Newstalk 106 from RTÉ, was the first producer of *Media Matters*. With only a week or so to go, we frenetically worked out a format for the programme. Our brief was to cover events in the media industries at home and abroad, our primary focus being journalism and reviews of how the main current affairs stories and other matters were treated each week.

Discussions on issues within journalism have continued to be a main feature on *Media Matters*. This has ranged from examining the huge growth in media organisations here over the past twenty years, to journalistic matters such as bias, balance and objectivity, changes in reporting styles, investigative journalism and the exponential increase in the art of spin and its practitioners. Programme contributors on these issues have included leading Irish media professionals, many of whom are represented in this book, and from abroad names such as John Pilger, Roy Greenslade, Ludovic Kennedy, Ray Snoddy and Alastair Campbell.

Over time *Media Matters* settled into its pattern, trial and error playing a major part in the programme's development. There were several changes of producer across all programmes in Newstalk, including *Media Matters*. When Jonathan moved to daily programming, the energetic Susan Cahill took over as producer.

Nearly two years ago my present producer, Paddy McDonnell, joined the programme and brought fresh thinking to our line-up. He and I tossed around various items for regular slots. I'd been keen on the idea of a series of interviews with prominent media professionals which would include film directors, television producers, radio and television presenters, newspaper editors and journalists. This 20-minute slot became "Under the Spotlight", and turned the tables, whereby the interviewers became the interviewees. Whereas these interviews combine both the personal and professional facets of each guest, they also cover their views on the broader issues within Irish media.

Media outlets in Ireland have mushroomed over the past twenty years. Ireland has seen major developments in broadcasting during this period from the rise of the "pirate" stations in defiance of the stodgy fare dished up at the time by the state broadcaster from its monopolistic ivory tower, to the introduction and spread of legitimate local radio stations throughout the country. These developments benefited both the broadcasting organisations and their listeners, who can now receive an alternative perspective on political and domestic affairs at local and national level. The introduction of texts and e-mail have brought a new listener participatory dimension to broadcasting. The increase in the number of music stations has led to a much wider and more diverse line-up of musical choice. But growth has produced another problem — whether or not there are now too many stations competing for listeners.

As the Broadcasting Commission of Ireland has increased the number of licences issued, so too has the worry of survival amongst established stations. Some are finding viability a problem, never mind turning in an annual profit which, at the end of the day, is the primary objective of any media organisation in the private sector. There is a mistaken belief that as the number of stations increases, so too does advertising revenue. Obviously this is not the case, as the advertising cake does not increase; it is merely carved into ever-diminishing slices. There is also criticism from some quarters that the number of speciality music licences will not attract sufficient listeners. A question frequently asked is whether it would have been more expedient to assign specialist music sections to the schedules of some of the new licences rather than an entire station schedule being devoted to, say, country music.

While radio broadcasting has increased in choice and developed in production values over the past two decades, in parallel print media has also expanded. Twenty-odd years ago the choice for Irish newspaper readers was restricted to *The Irish Times*, the Irish Independent Group of newspapers, the now defunct Irish Press Group, *The Cork Examiner* and some UK titles.

Over the years we've seen the introduction of Irish editions of the UK tabloids, the Irish *Star*, *Mirror* and *Sun*. Equally, the Irish magazine sector has grown in this period. True, several publications in this competitive sector have come and gone, but survivors such as *Magill* and *In Dublin* have battled on. *Magill* in particular has successfully risen from the ashes on a number of occasions.

And whilst on the topic of rising from the ashes, a major success has been *Phoenix* magazine which burst onto the Irish magazine publishing sector twenty or so years ago, developing its satirical and humorous take on Irish life and current affairs, and it has established a large and loyal readership.

Apart from the loss of all three Irish Press Group titles in this period, one particular favourite, *Hibernia*, went to its grave twenty or so years ago. Its unique formula has never really been replicated. Some would say a sinister element to the business of news media and its role in the democratic process has developed here, England and the US over this 20-year period but particularly within the last decade. Nowadays commonly referred to as "spin", the role of the public relations practitioner — or consultant as they prefer to be known — has developed in stature, control, power and in the skills of obfuscation employed by the "doctors". Twenty years ago who'd have thought a PR man — Alastair Campbell — would become a household name?

Many top journalists complain that the game of cat and mouse played between them and the spin doctors — political spin doctors in particular — has made reporting current affairs or obtaining access to politicians difficult and unsatisfactory. Increasingly, there are cases in Ireland, and in Britain, of political journalists being refused information or interview access if they have been deemed to be "off message".

The Freedom of Information Act is a misnomer because, many allege, it does precisely the opposite of what it is supposed to do. Civil servants and government officials are now very guarded when it comes to committing proposals, discussions or other matters to paper. Minutes of meetings and documents are written in a patois designed to destroy clarity and release only suitable or palatable information. Justine McCarthy, in her interview in this book, is particularly strong on this aspect of the communications chain.

Another development in media since the 1980s is the increase of the profile of journalists, many of whom are as much household names as the aforementioned Alastair Campbell, a journalist turned spin doctor. It is long accepted that television broadcast journalists, particularly anchors and chat show hosts, will obviously have a public profile — after all, the Gay Byrnes and Michael Parkinsons attained celebrity status long before the 1980s. But recent years have seen print and radio journalists (as opposed to presenters) climb the celebrity ladder as well. Today you'll frequently hear the words, "Did you read Kevin Myers today?" or "Did you see the piece by Miriam Lord?" Not so long ago it would have been "Did you see the article in the . . .?"

There has been much debate over the establishment of a Press Council in Ireland, as well as scarifying suggestions that this would be a government-appointed body. Media and public alike must resist such a development, the implications of which are obvious, not to mention frightening. This country needs a Press Council and many well-known people working in print media have welcomed the idea and they have stated that it should be in place for the protection of privacy rights and the individual. However, it must be a completely independent body in the interests of press freedom and the preservation of our democratic society.

This collection features the views of 17 leading Irish journalists interviewed in the "Under the Spotlight" series on these and many other media issues. Although they are all very different personalities, they do share many similarities. For instance, over half of them say that they drifted into journalism rather than setting out on a defined career path. The topics discussed range from the invasion of Iraq, to the arts, film production, Sinn Féin and the IRA, new ventures in publishing, alcoholism, national identity, the Tribunals, the Garda, planning corruption, the McCartney sisters and many more stories and prevalent issues that were "live" at the time of the interview. These conversations also embrace the interviewees' personal lives alongside their media work.

Each chapter in the book is a direct transcript of the recorded conversations with minimal editing to preserve the accuracy and context of what was said, so when reading this collection please bear in mind that people do not speak as they write.

Roger Greene
September 2005

C*onor* B*rady*

*I*n 1987 Conor Brady had the somewhat challenging privilege of taking over the editorship of The Irish Times *from the celebrated editor Douglas Gageby, who had been called back from his retirement to edit
the paper again in 1977 and salvage it from sliding into oblivion. At the
time of his appointment Conor Brady had held a number of distinguished
posts in Irish media, with two editorships to his name, those of the* Sunday Tribune *and the* Garda Review. *When Gageby finally retired from*
The Irish Times *there was much speculation as to who would succeed
him but it would appear that the deliberators were wasting their time as
Brady seems to have been the preferred choice all along. Significantly for
many, he was the first Catholic editor of that paper.*

RG: Was it a significant development being the first Catholic
editor of *The Irish Times*?

CB: I don't think so, really, in terms of the organisation itself. It was remarked upon at the time. But *The Irish Times*, by the late 1980s when I became editor, had moved well beyond those kind of issues. I think if I had been the wrong person for the job, then the fact that I was a Catholic would probably have been high-lighted a lot more strongly.

RG: Your predecessor was Douglas Gageby of course and he had two terms in that role. Was there a metamorphosis in *The Irish Times* under his editorship?

CB: Douglas took *The Irish Times* from 1964 through to 1974 and then again from 1977 through to 1987. So he had a very long tenure during a time of huge changes to Irish society. But he was a wonderful innovator, and he took *The Irish Times*, which was in terminal decline, and transformed it from being the in-house magazine of the Dublin Protestant middle and business classes — a shrinking body of people — and changed it into the required reading of the emerging Catholic, liberal, middle classes.

RG: You said that it was going badly and when Douglas Gageby was brought back again, it was a rescue job, and he made changes. But what did you face in 1987?

CB: Well I took over the paper in very good shape. I had been working closely with Douglas for years in the paper and, in fact, I was largely engaged in circulation-building. In a sense I under-stood how to keep the paper moving forward so there was a seamless transition at that point. There were difficulties though, in that there was a certain mystique about Douglas and people felt that the paper could not thrive under anybody other than Doug-las. Three of the previous four editorships had seen the paper in decline, let's put it that way. Douglas was the only person who had successfully edited the newspaper for any length of time since Bertie Smyllie. The other factor which was against me of course in the 1980s was that the economy was on its knees. Media always operates on the fringe of an economy, as you know. Advertising is a discretionary spend and newspapers are a discretionary spend. So it was a very tough time economically and I suppose the biggest problem I faced was the fact that the country was going down the tubes in terms of its economics.

RG: So advertising support was a bit thin on the ground?

CB: You can see it was very, very tight when you look at *The Irish Times* now and the size and scale of the paper. In my first summer as editor, 1987, the size of the paper was a standard 16 pages and I had to go to the Board to get 18 pages in for the summer months. Sixteen pages now would be half of one supplement!

RG: Well yes, even if you take the property section alone — in fact it is two sections now.

CB: The property section would be bigger now than the entire paper was at that time.

RG: In terms of circulation then, you obviously had to bring in the younger reader, as all newspapers do, so how did you go about that?

CB: There's a simple rule of thumb. Five per cent of a newspaper's readership die every year, so I was there for 16 years and I effectively renewed the readership and added a bit! The newspaper and the changes in Irish society were very much interlinked. It would be difficult to say which was the chicken and which was the egg. But of course the willingness of The Irish Times Trust to invest heavily in the paper enabled me to develop new services, new sections and gradually to expand the paper's appeal. That is the great thing about the Trust. Many harsh things were said about it over recent years, but the wonderful thing about it was that it did allow the resources to go back into the newspaper and at the same time protect the newspaper from takeover.

RG: And at that time, as well, you introduced a lot of young writers to the paper. People like Fintan O'Toole, for example, would have been one, as was Paddy Woodworth, John Waters and Michael Dwyer to name a few.

CB: Yes, it's difficult to look at some of them being young now as they're men and women of mature years. I was never so hung up on the youth thing in the paper. *The Irish Times* has never grown by talking down to young people or by, as it were, arguing down to them. It's almost an acquired taste. As young people come into maturity, take up positions in life and take up respon-sibilities, they find that they need the sort of judgement, the sort of information that a good, reasonably intelligent newspaper can give them. So they rise to it. We never really went for youth, as such. What we did do, and it was helpful and very significant, was that a great colleague of mine and a great loss to the paper, Christina Murphy, who died far too young, had worked very hard at building the newspaper in the schools with children and that, of course, planted a seed of awareness and a seed of under-standing. But then you would lose the readers from school, through college, through the early years of their career building, but then you'd pick them up as they matured and developed.

RG: Take us back to your beginnings. You grew up in Tullamore; tell us a bit about that.

CB: I have no family connections with that part of the world, although I call it home and I now have the great joy of having a little cottage in the Slieve Blooms where I sometimes go at week-ends. My father was the Garda Superintendent and my uncle was the local dispensary doctor, so between the uncle and the father there wasn't much going on that we didn't know about in the house. My father died when I was quite young, so then I went to boarding school in Roscrea and became involved in the school magazine; that was my first editorship, the school magazine in Roscrea. Then I went on to UCD where I became editor of *Campus UCD News*. So editing was there from the beginning I guess.

RG: You studied history and politics which is a classic degree for would-be journalists. At that stage had you made up your mind that you were going to work in journalism?

CB: I hadn't really, no. I wasn't really sure. I didn't know that there was a living to be had in journalism, to be quite honest, because there was very little of it in my family. I had some cousins on my mother's side, who worked in the *Independent* and in the old *Freeman's Journal*. But no, I had ideas of joining the Department of Foreign Affairs. That was one thing I was interested in. I also thought that I might go on to study architecture. But then I got a call from Ciaran Carty, who was the features editor of the *Sunday Independent* when I was in college, and he said, "Would you like to write a column for the *Sunday Independent*, writing about student news?" I said, "I would" and I did, and at the end of the month I got four cheques for five guineas each. I was as rich as Midas. I didn't know you got paid for doing this kind of thing and I said to myself, "Maybe there's a living to be had in this."

RG: You were for a time editor of the *Garda Review*; was that a legacy to your father's career?

CB: Perhaps an element of throwback, yes. It actually came about because when I went into *The Irish Times* as a young reporter, Donal Foley was the news editor — a great, legendary news editor — who came up to me and said, "What do you know about?" And I said, "Nothing really". Then he said, "Don't write about politics, they all want to write about politics. What does your father do?" So I told him what he was and he said, "Well, write about the Garda so." Now as it happened the Garda were going through a period of tremendous upheaval at that stage. They were very badly paid, there was a very harsh disciplinary system and nobody else in the paper was writing that story, so I wrote the story and came into contact with a man called Jack Marrinan who was the General Secretary of the Garda Representative Association. He was the first really professional union leader they had. He said to me, "Would you like to do the job of editing the *Garda Review*?" I thought it'd be a bit of fun, so I left *The Irish Times* to join the *Garda Review* and a lot of people at the time felt it was a retrograde career step.

RG: Well, that's what struck me looking at your CV.

CB: But I learned a huge amount. A good boarding school, UCD and *The Irish Times* are not exactly going to prepare you for the harsh realities of life. I learned more in the *Garda Review* in two years than I could have learned elsewhere, dealing with the Department of Justice, dealing with the bureaucracy, dealing with the Garda themselves, dealing with criminals, dealing with the prison service, dealing with lawyers, judges — it was a tremendously tough schooling. I also learned about design, layout and the importance of advertising in a publication. I learned that the man who actually brings the magazine out and puts it on the shelves in the shop is at least as important as the editor is. It also enabled me to go back to UCD and finish a post-graduate thesis which I wanted to do.

RG: You did an MA in what, history, politics?

CB: In politics.

RG: For a brief period you were in RTÉ. Did broadcasting appeal?

CB: It was after the *Garda Review*. Mike Burns, who was the head of the *News at One* Unit, as it was at the time, invited me and a few others to join. They were putting in extra news programmes so I did two years in radio which, again, was tremendous experience. I found it very trying, I must say. Live broadcasting is something which requires nerves of steel and I never found myself very comfortable with it. It took an awful lot out of me, but I enjoyed it immensely.

RG: Yes, it is relentless.

CB: Absolutely! It's a terrifying sensation when you're there and the red light goes on and you realise there's a million and a half people out there listening, or there used to be in those days. The potential to drop yourself into it is gigantic.

RG: But then the first real job, if I can call it that, as an editor of a national newspaper, was the *Sunday Tribune* in its early days, in the early eighties. What were your editorial objectives for a Sunday newspaper at that stage?

CB: I went back from RTÉ to *The Irish Times* and Douglas Gageby appointed me as a Deputy Editor. At the time I had in fact planned to go to Harvard to take the Nieman Fellowship in Journalism. I'd been nominated for that by the then American Ambassador Bill Shannon and I got a telephone call from Hugh McLaughlin who was the publisher of the *Sunday Tribune* who said, "Would you like to edit the *Sunday Tribune*?" which he, at that stage, owned along with John Mulcahy. I went to Gageby and I said to Douglas (I'd arranged to get leave to go to Harvard), "Now McLaughlin wants me to edit the *Sunday Tribune*." Douglas Gageby's reaction was, "You'd learn a hell of a sight more with the *Sunday Tribune* than you ever would in bloody Harvard." So I did the *Tribune* job for two years. The idea was to produce a quality Sunday newspaper, which *The Irish Times* wasn't doing or never has done, which was a great strategic error, I think. So I did it for two years and — I like to put it this way — the paper was a great success but the company was a failure. We did well. We had a circulation of 117,000 audited by Coopers Lybrand at the end, which was good considering *The Irish Times* was doing about 75,000 at the time. It was a very high circulation and it had the same ABC1 profile as *The Irish Times* and I believe that, had the investors been willing to stick with the project, I think it would have emerged as a hugely successful Sunday newspaper. Of course it would have meant that the landscape of the present Sunday newspaper market would not be what it is now.

RG: You've observed that radio broadcasting has its hazards but so too does being an editor of a national newspaper. What did you make of the recent debacle over Kevin Myers and the "bastards" issue, for want of a better expression?

CB: You're presenting me with a wonderful opportunity to keep my mouth shut.

RG: OK, well, can I let you off the hook a bit by asking what you would have done in that situation?

CB: I write for *Village* with Vincent Browne and I did write a piece there. I really feel that I wouldn't like to go any further than the paper's gone itself. The paper has acknowledged that it was wrong to publish the thing and I believe that is correct. I believe now that it should just be left behind and that the paper should move on.

RG: But the reality there, obviously, is that the onus is on the editor to see everything. Now we all know that it's virtually impossible for an editor to read every single item that goes in, but presumably, in an ideal world, an editor must look at all opinion and analysis pieces.

CB: Indeed, and in this case, as we know from the editor's account of events, that was done.

RG: It was done twice in fact.

CB: But it was a wrong call. It happens. I remember as editor I always had a very clear view of maintaining standards in the paper and that I could always forgive a wrong call because we all made them. I made them dozens of times each day. What I always found very difficult to forgive was a failure to observe procedure and a failure to adhere to procedure, because there are procedures in a good newspaper for the validation of copy and for measuring copy against the principles and the values of the paper. If those procedures are not adhered to and if they are recklessly cast aside, then I think an editor has to be very stern with the people he or she is dealing with.

RG: Talking of *Village*, you expressed concerns in the current edition, or rather the previous edition, about attributing quotes to their sources in articles and that it's now almost a requirement in US papers. But is this a beneficial development particularly when you look at, say, Watergate, when giant leaps of faith were taken and certainly, at the time, the only named source was "Deep Throat". Obviously we all know more now.

CB: Yes and until very recently, we believed "Deep Throat" may never have existed.

RG: Or was an amalgam of people, yes.

CB: I think that the point I was trying to make in that article was that the Americans can be far too literal about these things and they've now put in this ordinance which I think goes too far. The point I was making is that where non-attributable sources are used in a serious news report, I believe that an editor should always be across that. An editor should know who those sources are and should satisfy himself, or should, at the very least, say to the reporter, "I may not need to know your sources on this now, but, if it's challenged I may have to tell you to tell me who it is. Now, can you still write the story?" I did that in *The Irish Times* invariably and ninety nine times out of a hundred, it worked fine, but occasionally it meant that a story just slipped off the schedule.

RG: The profession of journalism, generally, in these islands, has it improved or deteriorated?

CB: I think it has done both. I think there is really excellent work being done by journalists, print, broadcast and web-based. You know, dealing with situations which are far more intractable and far more challenging than anything that had to be dealt with in previous generations. There's tremendous work being done on things like the tribunals and that. On the other hand, I do think that there are real pressures on journalists now which weren't there so much in the past. There's a pressure of productivity. A lot of them are employed on short-term contracts and they're asked to cover a whole range of things. I think there's very little opportunity for many of them to do anything really well with the result that there's a lot of work coming out which is, I think, slipshod, careless. Journalists don't make the calls, they don't check it out, they don't hear the other side of the story, sometimes by inclination and sometimes because they simply don't have the time or the resources to do it.

RG: Or they're on too many stories against deadlines.

CB: Yes; I'll give you an example of it. A couple of years back when I was in my last year in *The Irish Times*, we had a big restructuring thing to do and so the newspaper was being written about in other media quite a bit. I've a box of stuff at home and I think I must have about a hundred pieces in it written about *The Irish*

Times, about me, in which I'm quoted and so forth. I only got two telephone calls from journalists over that period. Everything else that's in those stories is gossip or rumour.

RG: But that is a very prevalent trait — not so much gossip and rumour, as the whole notion of comment and opinion in a news story which, as you know, the purists will tell you should never, ever be together.

CB: Indeed and in the case of *The Irish Times* it's specifically written into the articles of the Trust, which says that fact should be separated from opinion and opinion shall be responsibly based on known fact. These ordinances, in different ways, are applied in different media. There's a lot of shoddy work being done and there's a great lack of rigorous editorial supervision in many, many organisations, both print and broadcast.

RG: And it's happening in the UK papers as well, but not to the same degree. Here we're told how Bertie is feeling about an event that has taken place rather than just being told about the event.

CB: I don't worry too much about that I have to say. I think you can have a lot of opinion as long as it's clearly labelled as opinion. I think good, strong, vigorous argument is always included.

RG: No, I'm talking about how it finds its way into news stories.

CB: Oh, I see, finding its way into news, yes of course, I can only say I agree with you.

RG: Tell me, what are you doing now since you left *The Irish Times* in 2002. What have you been up to?

CB: I'm doing far too many things. I'm doing a book for Gill and Macmillan called *Up with the Times* which will look back over my sixteen years as editor. I teach media courses at the Graduate Business School in UCD — MBA and MBS courses. I have what is rather grandly referred to as a Visiting Professorship with the City University of New York, so I go over there from time to time.

RG: That sounds very posh!

CB: It sounds tremendously posh but the reality, I have to tell you, is quite different. The nice part about it is that they provide us with really great accommodation in New York, so it's a nice place to go and that was offered to me on a five-year basis, but I don't think I'm going to continue it for the five years. And then I'm still very much involved in the peace process in Northern Ireland which was something, I believed, had to be central to *The Irish Times* and its coverage. I've been involved for years in the British-Irish Association which does a lot of background communications between political parties and community groups in the North and I'm taking over as Chair of that in April.

RG: And that's a very active organisation?

CB: Very active, we've a small secretariat in London and we operate between Dublin, Belfast and London. Thomas Pakenham, the author, has been Chair for the past three years, so I'm taking over from Thomas in April and I'm looking forward to that.

$\mathcal{F}$rank $\mathcal{C}$onnolly

$\mathcal{F}$rank Connolly is an investigative journalist whose work with The Sunday Business Post and other media outlets contributed to the establishment of two judicial tribunals — the Flood (now Mahon) Tribunal into Planning and Payments and the Morris Tribunal into allegations of Garda corruption in Donegal. Over a lengthy career in journalism he has also been responsible for breaking many important news stories that have had a significant impact on Irish political, social and business life. Describing Frank Connolly as a heavyweight investigative journalist is almost inadequate. In a world where true investigative reporting has dwindled at home and abroad, Frank has battled on and brought to the Irish public stories of a magnitude unequalled in the Irish media in recent years. For example, in 1988 he wrote about Ray Burke's alleged involvement in planning corruption. He has provided in-depth stories behind the Mahon tribunal and has written extensively about

Garda corruption in Donegal and interviewed the McBrearty family.
He's been a regular commentator on the North and has worked for or-
ganisations such as RTÉ, Magill, The Sunday Business Post, Ireland
on Sunday, *CNN,* TV3, Sunday Tribune *and of course he's a regular*
contributor to Newstalk 106. This interview with Frank was recorded on
the day the IRA issued its statement on the cessation of all military ac-
tivities.

RG: You've a lengthy CV in journalism, particularly investigative journalism, so what is your personal motivation behind this
area of work?

FC: Well as much as I would have a personal motivation, I
think from the very beginning when I went into research and then
journalism in my early twenties, I always had a view that journalists have a responsibility to highlight the needs and wants of the
people who are dispossessed or the people who don't have
power. Equally I think I also developed a view in later years that
it wasn't just enough to expose the abuses of people's human
rights or to highlight social inequalities or to highlight the problems faced by people who have fewer resources than others. I
think it also became apparent to me that one of the most important things about journalism is to expose the activities of the powerful and the manner in which very powerful people in society,
whether it be in politics or business or financial or other areas of
life, often abuse those powers.

RG: So has this come from a sense of concern over injustice or
could any of it be linked to your upbringing, your formative
years?

FC: My parents were both very committed to human rights
and to justice. My father Frank worked in the ESB for most of his
life and had been a teacher before that and my mother Madeleine
has been a tireless campaigner on a lot of social issues — the

Travellers' issue and the rights of disabled people, the rights of children. So there was a certain influence there. I think at university I certainly developed that through studying sociology, history and politics which I did in Trinity. Of course at that time I think that particularly the social sciences and sociology were an ideological debate as much as anything else: how society changes, how society should change, how different forces prevent or facilitate change in society. I think that was obviously an influence as well.

RG: And presumably, from your perspective, you would say that the media plays a major role in the changes in society?

FC: Yes, although at that time I wasn't particularly wedded to the view that I would be a journalist or anything like that. In fact I was active in university in students' union-type activities — and in sport as well! Those days in the seventies were days of revolutionary fervour, I suppose you could say, where everybody wanted to change things immediately, or yesterday! I was involved in that respect in college politics. I also developed a lot of interest in what you would call individual campaigns or campaigns for social justice while I was a student. I've ended up in journalism almost by accident. I was doing post-graduate studies and then I ended up in the west of Ireland doing research and I applied for a job with RTÉ when it came up and got the job through competition.

RG: One of the jobs you had within RTÉ was as a researcher on *The Late Late Show* and that was in the mid- to late seventies and the early eighties. How did you find that? Was it a gratifying experience or did you feel it wasn't sufficiently serious journalistically?

FC: Well I think *The Late Late Show* in itself is an amazing journalistic experience for any young person. I was a researcher on the programme for a year and I think I was fortunate in that Gay

Byrne, who was producer of the programme at the time, asked me to concentrate on two single hour programmes. In other words, I didn't do the week-in, week-out stuff. One programme dealt with Dublin's inner city and its people and the second programme dealt with the ongoing debate about nuclear power in which I was particularly interested. I was part of a larger movement trying to stop the construction of a nuclear power station in Carnsore in Wexford at the time. So I had a very good year with the *Late Late*. I also worked on other programmes on the radio, morning programmes and current affairs programmes, so it was a very interesting experience.

RG: At what stage did you decide to forsake RTÉ to go into journalism, mostly in print, which has been your career until very recently?

FC: There were a couple of factors. There was, at that time, an atmosphere in RTÉ which was not conducive to certain types of programmes or certain types of politics, if I could put it that way. Particularly because of the way things in the North were breaking out — this is just in the period leading up to the hunger strikes — there were very, very fraught debates and arguments about what was happening within RTÉ. It was like a maelstrom of political debate and argument. I think Section 31 of the Broadcasting Act had a very, very negative influence on programme makers in RTÉ. So that was one issue that was particularly important.

RG: Sure, but at that stage, as we know, RTÉ had a lot of accusations levelled at it that it was, perhaps, sympathetic to the republican movement and that its reporting was imbalanced. Was that your experience?

FC: I think it was the contrary. Any attempt to make programmes that brought to light or brought to audiences in the South what actually was happening in the North, brought with it accusations that you were in some way sympathetic to the IRA or to Sinn Féin which was banned from the airwaves. In hindsight it was an absolutely ludicrous situation where journalists, who were trying to expose what was going on in the country, couldn't deal with arguably the most important issue at the time. But that was only one issue. I actually wanted to get into print journalism from an early stage and I went on from there in the early eighties to work as a freelance for a number of publications.

RG: So at what stage did you decide to set about unveiling corruption in the country? When did that ambition surface?

FC: Well I noticed that when I was doing freelance work — and I worked extensively, almost full-time, with some newspapers: the *Sunday Tribune, Magill,* I worked for the *Irish Press* as an inside report writer on a daily basis — and a lot of the stories that I was doing for them and the *Sunday Press* at the time were about corruption-related issues. But they were more to do with, as I say, highlighting miscarriages of justice and socially related stories. It was only when I joined *The Sunday Business Post* in the early nineties and worked full-time with Damien Kiberd — one of your colleagues here, but then editor of the *Business Post* — and because of the nature of the paper which was aimed at business people, at a particular niche market, he encouraged me to look at that side of it and the relationship between business and politics, which is that interface where the seeds of corruption are sown.

RG: But you had already had some experience of that in *Magill* as you've mentioned and one of the stories — which perhaps you could outline how you went about getting it — was the Ray Burke story and alleged corruption in planning.

FC: Well, that's right; in the eighties, I think it was 1988, I did an investigation of allegations of planning corruption in north Dublin and these allegations were focused around Ray Burke and

a number of people, people close to him that he'd appointed to
very important positions within the planning structures. And of
course, there were also questions about the then Assistant City
Manager, George Redmond. The issue at stake here was the manner in which people were being paid huge amounts, millions of
pounds of compensation after being refused planning permission
at the time and that raised all sorts of questions and loopholes in
the law that facilitated people, whom we now know, were acting
in a very corrupt fashion — builders, politicians and public officials.

RG: You were talking of the alleged corruption with regard to
planning in north Dublin. One of the people you interviewed, in
Zimbabwe in fact, was Patrick Gallagher who, as we all know
now, was one of Charles Haughey's benefactors.

FC: Yes, I got the opportunity to interview Patrick Gallagher
who was living there having come out of prison. If you remember,
he spent some time in jail in the North in relation to the Merchant
Banking affair and he ended up heading off to South Africa and
Zimbabwe subsequently. However it worked out, I was told,
through somebody close to me who knew Patrick Gallagher, that
he had information relevant to the stuff that was emerging in public at the time, about payments to Charles Haughey. We took a
risk really and I went off for three or four days or almost a week
to Zimbabwe and interviewed him over a period of two or three
days. It was only on the very last day, for whatever reason, that he
dropped this bombshell, after I had spent hours and hours with
him talking about every single issue under the sun. He told me
about the day Charlie Haughey had been made leader of Fianna
Fáil and was about to become Taoiseach back in 1979. He had
been called out with his younger brother to Kinsealy and arrived
to find the prospective ministers waiting to be appointed by the
Boss or the leader of the party. He (Patrick Gallagher) was called

in ahead of them and he was told by Mr Haughey that he, the incoming Taoiseach, had financial problems. Paddy Gallagher after "toing and froing" for a while, asked him how much was the damage and how much did he owe and he said he'd pay out half of it, which was about £375,000.

RG: And he demanded that in fairly colourful language too, as we recently learned.

FC: I think Paddy Gallagher is well capable of colouring a story himself, he's quite a colourful individual. But I think that was a very important revelation because, for the first time, it was a businessman saying that he had effectively financed Charles Haughey. Now his explanation was that he felt that Haughey was like Irish royalty and that he had to look after the nation. He was a visionary and a statesman and he shouldn't have to bother about how to pay his bills. As we now know, Charles Haughey's bills were very expensive on a monthly basis, but Gallagher and these people claimed that they got no benefit from this act of benevolence to Mr Haughey.

RG: But in fact the Gallagher family, particularly Patrick's father, Matt Gallagher, was a long-time associate, both in business and socially, of Mr Haughey.

FC: Well that's absolutely right. In fact Gallagher helped Haughey purchase a large house in Edenmore which Gallagher then bought off Haughey and developed for housing. A lot of Raheny and that part of north Dublin was built by the Gallaghers and of course Matt Gallagher identified another house for Haughey in Kinsealy and a stud farm that Haughey invested in. So Matt Gallagher in fact gave Haughey a very significant leg-up at a very important time in his career.

RG: Moving on, you were the first to write a detailed report of the Brian Keenan kidnapping. How did that come about?

FC: I knew friends of Brian Keenan. In fact a college friend of mine was very close to him in Belfast and through that connection I got involved when Brian was kidnapped in the Lebanon in the late eighties and really just helped his family, his two sisters in particular, to raise the issue in Dublin. These people came from a loyalist background, a working-class unionist background in Belfast and had never really spent any time in the south, never mind the halls of power in Dublin. I suppose I just used my journalistic connections to bring and introduce them to politicians, media people and other people who might help to raise a very, very important issue of an Irish citizen who was literally sitting in a blindfold in some cell in the Lebanon. I think the perception — and indeed the fact — was that very little was being done for him even though he was a dual passport holder; he held both British and Irish passports. So I think the fact that the British government were doing very little because they were, in a sense, players in the region, in the conflict in the region, whereas the Irish government had a little bit more credibility. I think that by highlighting his Irish background and by pushing the Department of Foreign Affairs in particular to make an issue of his case, I think it probably, if anything, helped to facilitate an earlier release than some of the other hostages, who were mainly American and British.

RG: Frank, for a while you were Northern Editor of *The Sunday Business Post* so what are your thoughts on the statement in relation to the cessation of military action by the IRA?

FC: I think it's been a long time coming. I'm not surprised that it did come and I think that for a long time it was an inevitable consequence of the peace process, going as far back as the early nineties, if not the late eighties. As it turns out, that peace process started at the time I joined the *Business Post*, so I think we were able to make a significant contribution to the political debate at the time. I interviewed, during those years leading up to the first ceasefire in 1994, all of the major players, unionist, nationalist, republican, senior British politicians, including the then Prime Minister, senior Irish politicians, and Albert Reynolds who was Taoiseach at a crucial time. We ran question-and-answer interviews over a period of months which helped to expose the issues that were both dividing and uniting the politicians. Obviously the IRA's initiatives during that period were very significant and had a huge role in driving the thing forward. I think that because there is no point in re-hashing the arguments, the fact is that the Good Friday Agreement emerged from that and we were still, several years later, waiting for that agreement to be implemented. I think this is probably one of the most important contributions to ensure this agreement is finally implemented. I think it will be some time yet before that process is completed, but I think this is a huge and historic step in that direction.

RG: You say it's a long time coming, with which I think most people would agree, but do you think its wording is sufficiently clear?

FC: Well everybody is coming from their own background and views on this. I mean, from the point of view of watching the republicans over a long period of time, I think where they say in the statement that "volunteers must not engage in any other activities whatsoever and assist the development of purely political and democratic programmes through exclusively peaceful means". I can't see how you can get it any more definitive than that.

RG: But it is very, very broad.

FC: I think it's broad but it's also avoiding any — and I think people will leap all over this particular bit — acknowledgement that the IRA has ever been involved in criminal activities and yet it's also stating to the wider world that they're not going to tolerate, or that their members or volunteers are not going to engage in, any of that sort of activity.

RG: So, broadly welcomed by most people. Now, staying in the north of the country geographically, the revelations from the Morris Tribunal were staggering. What do you believe should be done about Garda corruption in regard to a regulatory, overseeing body?

FC: I think I've said it quite a lot because I've been interviewed as a result of my journalism in Donegal. The fact that we were the first people to write, both in *The Sunday Business Post* and then on television programmes on TV3, about the corruption and the mistreatment of citizens in Donegal by members of the force. I think the only way of, if not preventing at least helping to prevent, this type of abuse of power, is by having some sort of independent ombudsman who can have sufficient powers to investigate allegations of wrongdoing by members of the Garda. The reason it's so important is because the Garda already have huge powers and they have a huge influence over the lives of citizens. I believe the problem is that a culture has built up where power has been abused and it's been abused in ways that are not just about harassing young people on the streets for no reason. It's actually a culture that's got into the management and the senior structures of the force over many, many years and there are a lot of reasons for it, not least the fact of the political conflict on the island which has allowed power to be centralised, for reasons that were probably logical at the time, but that have a downside now. So I think that there has to be some sort of independent structure and the Patten Report is probably the best road map as to how that can work itself out through the functioning of an ombudsman.

RG: Finally, the Monica Leech PR consultancy fee retainer by Martin Cullen appeared to be one of the most lucrative in the history of public relations. Was it satisfactorily explained in your view, by Cullen and the Department?

FC: Well I wrote that story and got quite a lot of flak from the Minister as a result of it. The fact of the matter is we went to ask a simple question: what did this woman, who happened to be a constituent, a close advisor and a friend of Mr Cullen, do to deserve a €400,000 consultancy payment over, whatever it was, eighteen months or two years? She didn't have any significant organisation. She didn't have any staff, she didn't appear to have any other major contracts, yet she was getting this very, very large retainer or payment for her consultancy work. She was travelling all around the world with the Minister and I don't think it was adequately explained. I don't think the Quigley Report, which was set up to investigate it, dealt with all of the issues and I certainly think it says an awful lot that the Standards in Public Office Commission, which apparently wanted to investigate it, said that they didn't have sufficient powers to do a proper inquiry or investigation. I think that's a very damning indictment of our structures.

RG: Now you've joined the Centre for Public Inquiry. What are its functions and what is your role specifically?

FC: I'm the Executive Director of this Centre which is set up to carry on what's known as public interest journalism, using the skills of investigative journalism to highlight issues of public concern right across the board. We have a sort of a road map of things we want to inquire into and report on over the next five or six years. We have funding provided by Atlantic Philanthropies for a five-year programme and we're also responding to things brought to us by ordinary citizens to do with maladministration or mistreatments by agencies of the state or by public bodies or officials.

So it's really using or providing the skills of journalism and using them to highlight issues and matters of public concern.

RG: And was this the reason you left *Ireland on Sunday* to join this agency?

FC: Yes. We were discussing it for a while with the funding agency and eventually they agreed that they would put forward a package and I approached a number of people including Feargus Flood, the former Chairman of the Planning and Payments Tribunal, to chair the new body and we've been up and running since early this year.

*E*amon *D*elaney

E amon Delaney has been a diplomat, author, journalist, broadcaster
and, more recently, the editor of **Magill** *magazine. His personal
memoir of working in the Department of Foreign Affairs,* **The Accidental Diplomat,** *catapulted him to public recognition in this country when
it was first published a few years ago. For the most part it is a humorous
account of his years in the Department of Foreign Affairs and his postings to New York and Washington, amongst others. He was branded a
cynic and accused of not being a "true player" by the Department of
Foreign Affairs when the book was first published. At the time of its publication, he was on leave from the Civil Service, and never returned.*

RG: You started your career working for a company called
Commercial Information. What was that all about?

ED: That was in the early eighties. Commercial Information published a series of small trade publications but given the recessionary times, it was actually very successful and went on to become a whole bunch of other companies. They were successful in terms of media marketing, corporate image and all of that kind of thing. A chap called Paddy Hayes was the main publisher and I worked on reports to do with offshore drilling, mining in Ireland and the energy industry. So for a chap of 17, who had yet to go to college, I worked there for two years and it was a great grounding in journalism.

RG: So before you went to college, you were working as a journalist, albeit on trade publications.

ED: Precisely; I was a member of the NUJ, the publications and PR branch as it then was, and it was a full-time job, reporting, putting the magazines together, compiling directories and so on. I then thought that this was too early to have a proper job. I decided to travel the world, went off for a year and when I came back I went to college for three years.

RG: Which college?

ED: I went to UCD.

RG: And what did you study there?

ED: I studied English and History, a great combination. It was great for me at the time. I was very enthusiastic; we had great teachers: Declan Kiberd, Seamus Deane . . .

RG: . . . and Gus Martin?

ED: Yes, I was reading Gus Martin only last night in a 1963 *Studies* magazine. Yes, great characters and I loved college. I was very involved in the debating culture, and I was auditor of the

L&H, the college debating society. I think it's always a good thing to come to college a little bit late. I'd sown my wild oats, if you like, and then got stuck down to the books.

RG: So you took on college with a degree of maturity and you weren't out looking for the *craic* like the majority of students who start at the age of 18. What age were you when you started your degree?

ED: I would have been 20 or 21. I then did a one-year MA in English which I didn't really finish, the usual story. I was knocking around Dublin for a year in '87, '88, and then I joined the Civil Service.

RG: When you were in college had you any idea in your head about what you wanted to do, because the title of your book is *The Accidental Diplomat* — was that how you ended up in the Civil Service, by accident?

ED: It sort of is. To be honest, what I really wanted to do, in a half-formed idea in my heart or brain, was to be a writer and that still is there. I'd already started writing fiction with, in the back of my mind, thinking of doing journalism as well. But I neglected to do journalism as such and in college I didn't pursue any of the journalistic activities. I was also very interested in politics and international relations, so when a vacancy in Foreign Affairs came up, I applied for it. Later in my career, I realised it was an accidental profession but even when I started I thought that too. I foresaw myself as a sort of Graham Greene figure, writing novels while going round the world.

RG: You saw yourself in a white suit in the Caribbean!

ED: Precisely, tapping away and maybe writing prose journalism and fiction. There's a great Irish tradition in that lifestyle. So I joined the Department of Foreign Affairs and once you're in it, you're in it.

RG: But did you have any ambitions in that direction when you were in college?

ED: Not as such, no, but as I pointed out in the book, the Civil Service does take liquorice all sorts, if you like. It takes people who have an artistic sensibility, people who are legalistic, who are economic. By its nature, it almost has mavericks. So you can retain an interest in media or international relations or whatever or cultural interests and also be in the Civil Service at the same time.

RG: Did you get a sense of career fulfilment from it or was there an element of drudgery?

ED: There was an element of drudgery, certainly. When the foreign postings come up — that's why you join it, for the foreign postings — I applied, I think, for India, which was an exciting prospect, but I didn't get it. I got New York, which was fantastic. I was there three years and I worked in the United Nations and the Irish Consulate in New York. Then, any sense of the drudgery of it, which is always still there, was very much blighted out of the way because I was having such an interesting time, culturally and so on.

RG: So having got a posting to New York, you subsequently went to Washington, didn't you?

ED: Yes, I went to Washington for nearly half a year after that, which was great.

RG: But surely that signalled some form of acclaim, in terms of your abilities as a diplomat in the Foreign Service?

ED: I think it was felt that I was certainly a "people" person. I was good at the social whirl — the Irish-American circuit, which is a tricky one, culturally and politically, but I was very good at that and I embraced it.

RG: Tricky in what way?

ED: It's a form of Irish culture which is like a time capsule of the 1950s or 1960s. We have moved way on. It's very nationalistic.

RG: Sort of Kennedy-driven, is it?

ED: Oh, beyond, it's kind of IRA supporters. In some sense it's very conservative, very out of touch with modern Ireland.

RG: Presumably you came in touch with organisations like Noraid, did you? So how did you find it, how did you find what they were espousing at the time?

ED: I found it was best to not go in there with a big stick because that had been done in the eighties by the Irish government and diplomats and it had had a counter-productive effect. I thought it was better to work with them on the basis that — perhaps it is patronising to say it — but they were just mistaken and misguided in understanding Ireland and Northern Ireland and where we were coming from. I had a few hairy encounters. In *Magill*, now, we revisit this territory. We've just written a piece about Peter King, a Congressman in Long Island. People like him who never, ever visit Ireland or have nothing to do with the conflict and give their support to organisations linked to violence.

RG: Is their naivety as overt as we think?

ED: I think it is because he's a politician and he would know the ropes close to Sinn Féin. But I was meeting people who could not name the six counties.

RG: And there's plenty up there that can't either . . .

ED: Or down here indeed! No, it was kind of instinctual, it was in their DNA, historically, as Irish-Americans. They'd come there through waves of emigration born out of political conflicts.

RG: And still living on the eighteenth- and nineteenth-century stories, that are perpetuated over and over again.

ED: But there were other cultural gaps as well and these have been accentuated since I was there. Ireland is now popular culture, multicultural, very pro-economic with all the characteristics that Americans should love as a philosophy, but the Connemara donkeys and traditional music and that version of Ireland has gone on, so the descendants of Irish emigrants in America have been a bit left behind.

RG: Coming back to your work in Washington and New York, how close were you to US politics and US politicians?

ED: When I was there it was before the period of American hands-on engagement with Ireland and with Northern Ireland. It has to be said I was there for the last time of George Bush senior's regime, before Clinton, before the peace process as well. So there was a sense that we were well got with American politicians but nothing as intense and close as it became later with the peace process. Nevertheless, Ireland has had a great "in" and cache with American political culture through the diaspora. The Irish are the first urban proletariat in America. They came after the Germans. They formed the cities and the towns. They stayed away from the land for good reason. So because the Irish embassies are quite small, other embassies are much larger and have military attachés, but because we were quite small, we had an intimacy and involvement which was nice.

RG: What about looking for the Irish vote in terms of US politicians, presumably you were approached to help in that regard?

ED: A little bit. The Irish vote is broken down now because Irish-Americans have become more prosperous, more conservative and have gone to the Republicans from the Democrats. I tell a story in the book about Ted Kennedy, who was under quite a bit of pressure two elections back in Massachusetts and he needed some help. He needed some appearances by Irish government ministers and strangely enough didn't they all start to coincidentally appear in his constituency around the time of the election or just before. We supplied some material that then became his speech, which we would then respond to. It was quite duplicitous actually. But there was quite a bit of intimacy there, particularly with the likes of Ted Kennedy.

RG: When you actually came back from New York and Washington, were you still in the Civil Service at that stage or did you leave to write *The Accidental Diplomat*?

ED: When I came back I worked for two years here and I was in the Northern Ireland division, which was very exciting and that formed part of the material for the book. I came back in '93 when the peace process was kicking in and Albert Reynolds was Taoiseach. So I kept a diary, to be honest, Roger, and I drew from the diary quite extensively for the book, which I know is quite a bold thing to do, but there you go. That became the serious part of the book, the rest of the book is less serious, with more comedy. I still had an idea that I was not going to stay in Foreign Affairs for life. In the same period I was working on the novel I wrote, *The Casting of Mr O'Shaughnessy*, which was a black comedy about history, nationalism and commemoration which draws upon some of the issues that keep conflicts like Northern Ireland alive. That was getting close to publication. Bloomsbury in the UK had agreed to publish it, which was exciting, and they launched it in 1995. I was thinking of taking a career break but what forced my hand was another posting was coming up — Buenos Aires, which I thought was exciting and I imagined sunny beaches, hanging out with Diego Maradona and his friends, nightclubs and all the rest of it. But I got Luxembourg — as someone said, "The bright lights of Luxembourg — all three of them." So I thought, "God is sending me a signal here — or maybe the personnel section of Foreign Affairs is sending me a signal." So I decided to take a career break. The book was published during the career break and then I began a period of freelance journalism. But to get back to the North, I did two full years there and that formed a lot of my views and philosophies on the North on top of the views I already had.

RG: So you took the career break because you turned down Luxembourg and then wrote *The Accidental Diplomat*. Surely, given the tone of it, the humour in it and the fact that it was basically a piss-take, did you really expect that you'd be accepted when you went back or if you went back to Foreign Affairs?

ED: I didn't tell them it was coming, obviously, and it was great fun when it came out. This is known as elaborately burning one's boats or bridges or both. I actually extended the career break. They were tremendously generous. It's a wonderful facility that the Civil Service has because you can extend a career break from one year to two years and up to five. But there was no question of my ever going back after the book was published. And there was one other, rather childish matter.

RG: Which was?

ED: It was related to the *O'Shaughnessy* book. I had, as a prank under a pseudonym, written to the then Taoiseach, Charles J. Haughey, looking for medals for having fought in the War of Independence and had got them. I publicised this a few years ago when the paperback edition of *O'Shaughnessy* came out. I had an idea that this was going to come to light and I thought it would be as well to have parted cleanly from the Civil Service before the story broke.

RG: But presumably all of this was regarded as being somewhat irreverent. What kind of flak did you get after the publication and the fact that the book itself was well received?

ED: I think you put your finger on it there because the fact that it was well received and given credibility really infuriated them. They had no idea the book was coming out. I didn't realise how big it was going to be in terms of publicity. It was serialised in the *Sunday Times* and then it appeared in *The Irish Times* magazine on the Saturday. But even before that, the six o'clock news on RTÉ did an item on it and immediately the phones started ringing from Stockholm where the European summit was on at the time. My former colleagues rang and said, "Eamon, what's this about you writing a book?" and I said, "Well, it's coming out and it's just a humorous tale." They were laughing. But there was one character, I won't name him, but he'll probably never talk to me again for the rest of his life. He's a senior figure and resourceful for stories. He rang me and said, "I'll get the book and I'll ring you right back." I've never heard from him since. When the book came out, it was seized upon. People loved it. Irish people love a story, particularly one from behind the scenes. Foreign Affairs then decided to do a strange thing, or a wise thing, and just ignore it and let it go. But as it went on and on and then I had an hour on Marian Finucane and that particularly infuriated them and they did things the wrong way round. Sean Ó hUigínn, the Irish Ambassador in Washington, was home on leave and he, at his own invitation, went on to the radio programme to rebut the book and this only gave it more legs.

RG: Just what you wanted.

ED: Yes, and meanwhile there was a kind of a spin by diplomats who, whenever they met journalists, were consistent in saying, "Delaney wasn't really a player. He has an axe to grind. It's
all funny-funny and doesn't mean anything."

RG: I think you were branded a cynic at the time. After the
book came out, presumably you then resigned. Was it worrying
leaving the security of the Civil Service to become a freelance
journalist? You'd have been ideally positioned to have become a
pol. corr. for, say, *The Irish Times*.

ED: I probably would have been. Strangely, I didn't get directly involved in journalism after that; something I regret actually. I know it sounds like a silly regret but I still had the idea that
I wanted to write "The Novel". So I went to Paris for a couple of
months and finished a Celtic Tiger contemporary novel that was
really quite flat and has been put in the bottom of the wardrobe.
In that time I probably should have been off developing media
expertise on the back of the book. I found myself telling a lot of
the same stories from the book. However, I did do a lot of journalism. I did a lot of lifestyle things, I did book reviews for *The Irish
Times* and I started writing for American publications, *The Publishers' Weekly* based in New York, Condé Nast Publications and then
a regular bit with the *Herald* doing a lot of punditry. I liked that
because I got a lot off my chest that I had strong feelings about.

RG: And how are you finding your present position today as
the editor of *Magill*, which did the phoenix act about a year ago
with yourself and Ian Hyland. How's that been going?

ED: It's going very well, it really has. It's bedded down now.
We're almost a full year on and it was always problematic. It took
a lot of work to get it back but we're really happy that we've

completely redesigned the magazine and we also re-shaped it. We gave it a sort of right-of-centre focus, which has been a strong identity for it. It's not universally like that. We have dissonant voices but it's always provocative and interesting. But the great thing is that we have younger journalists; new people, new voices — not shaped by the politics or ideas of an older generation but by new ideas and by globalisation and the international scene — are coming flocking to us to write, which is great.

RG: Well, of course, you're competing on a monthly basis with what is happening in *The Irish Times* or the *Irish Independent* for that matter, not forgetting the UK qualities. It must be difficult though, to come up with a decent editorial policy, particularly as *Magill* has had an ideology that was left-of-centre until you came along. Did that end up being a criticism that you accepted or rejected?

ED: No, I relish that kind of polarisation. I'm not making anything up, but on the street here before I came in, a young business fellow in a shirt and tie grabbed me and said, "You're the *Magill* editor. Well done, it's great to have an alternative voice." He's the kind of person we're trying to appeal to. I've been in radio debates with people like Fintan O'Toole who say, probably correctly, "Why is it so different when the *Herald*, the *Indo*, the *Star* all take a sort of right-of-centre perspective as well?" But looking at all media, access to RTÉ or *The Irish Times* is very influential in terms of opinion-forming. This middle class liberalism informs, has a lot of ideas and says, "This is an issue but there's a contrary way to look at it."

RG: Just before we finish up, Eamon, and continuing with middle-class liberalism, how do you think *The Irish Times* has shaped up since Conor Brady was editor?

ED: I had this discussion this morning with somebody who works for *The Irish Times*. I think it's going in the right direction, I really do. I think Geraldine Kennedy has identified that there is a dilemma, that *The Irish Times* is out of step with the Irish people it's selling to. They've got a lot of things completely wrong, like the citizenship referendum; being rabidly anti-Bush during the election (and still are); they've a certain perspective on the Middle East, not shared by great amounts of Irish people. Also there's a huge schizophrenia there, or disparity between the editorial policy and these rather robust, capitalistic property supplements, motoring, children's clothes at the weekend and dining. I think Geraldine Kennedy has kind of identified that there is a dichotomy there and it needs to be addressed or one needs to move in tandem with the other. I have to say also that I find it a bit rich when I see Conor Brady, former editor, writing in *Village* criticising the direction of *The Irish Times* when he presided over the former *Irish Times'* woolly, left-of-centre "I'm very affluent but I feel good because I say these things" sort of approach. Sorry, that was a bit of a rant there.

RG: No, it was a decent enough rant, because when you look at it from an ideological viewpoint, there is this equation — it started in Europe and Blair has adopted it mostly because of Will Hutton and his writings — that just because you're left-wing doesn't mean that you can't have money, have accoutrements and be acquisitive. But you're obviously more of the old school there, are you?

ED: No, not really, I absolutely agree with you there. The French, for example — Mitterrand saw himself as a socialist, but had a nice lifestyle and had a great interest in the arts and culture. I particularly like that. You know this phrase, "I do right but I say left"? *The Irish Times* would robustly support the property culture, renting, and yet if they wrote enough articles about travellers in a totally one-sided way, you have this feel good factor. It's a sort of Mary Robinson-type of socialism. Give me Pat Rabbitte or Eamon Gilmore any day.

RG: Or don't tell me John Prescott . . .

ED: Yes, but really it's just infuriating. It's a kind of PC-ness with *The Irish Times*. Look at *The Guardian* for example, which has faced the same dilemma, and *The Guardian* is fairly similar to *The Irish Times* but in the UK context. I would read *The Guardian* a lot and through their books section you see much more consistency. They know there's that dilemma.

Eamon Dunphy

L *ove him or hate him, he has left his imprint on the nation, as a footballer in the sixties and then, increasingly into the seventies, he showed a gift for telling it as it is in his writing. Those on the wrong end of a tackle from him, be it in the* Sunday Independent *or on his* Last Word *programme on Today FM in the past or now on his breakfast show on Newstalk 106, stagger from the encounter both shaken and stirred. Eamon Dunphy has proved time and again that he's an engaging writer, not just in newspapers but also in his biographies of U2 and Roy Keane for example. He is forthright in his views and seemingly fearless of the consequences. Is he a self-contained loner or, like the rest of us, vulnerable? When I began the interview I wasn't sure and, come to think of it, I was no wiser at the end.*

RG: Eamon, what brought you into writing after your football career?

ED: Well towards the end of my less-than-glorious football career, I realised that I'd have to do something afterwards and I didn't have any other skills, so I began to write the odd column for newspapers — *The Observer* and *The Sunday Times* — about football. Then I wrote a book, an autobiographical memoir, about six months towards the end of my career and really football books at that stage were very banal and mostly ghosted. I did this myself and it wasn't a story of success. It wasn't a happy-clappy story, it was a rather sad story and it was well received. I thought that the only asset I had was my knowledge of soccer and I set out to try and become a football writer.

RG: You mentioned your memoir, so for those listeners who haven't read it, can you take us back to your childhood, growing up and school?

ED: I went to school in Drumcondra, a very good school, St Patrick's National School, and one year in secondary school followed. There was a very good library in Drumcondra and I was a very hungry reader from an early age. In those days I think you had to keep your books for two weeks before you could change them. You got two books and I always used to be up there the next day looking to see if I could fiddle out a few more books. So I read a huge amount of books when I was a kid. I also read my father's newspapers. When he'd come home at night I'd grab them from him. He was a big newspaper reader. So I was always a huge reader.

RG: And this was from the age of ten or so?

ED: No, from the age of seven, six, five even, because we didn't have television in those days and I had to amuse myself in some way and it took me into a new imaginative sphere. I read about all kinds of things, not just sport, but politics, wars, all kinds of stuff. At the time I was just amusing myself and escaping, but when I got older, I never lost the habit of reading newspapers and books. So, by the time I was 27 or 28, I had inadvertently acquired a huge store of words and had fertilised, if you like, my imagination. It was a big help when I began to write myself.

RG: And that was irrespective of any encouragement from teachers in school. It was something within yourself?

ED: Yes, it was. I had a very good teacher in my school, a man called Mr Hayden, who was a delightful man and a great encouragement to me because I was a shy and rather timid young fellow and he was always a help, because he encouraged me all the time to believe I was worthwhile, which is important to a young person.

RG: You developed a fearsome reputation in the *Sunday Independent*. Were you told to be that aggressive or was it just something that you did automatically?

ED: They couldn't hold me back, Roger! I started my career as a journalist in the first *Sunday Tribune*, which Conor Brady edited. I went in there as the soccer correspondent and immediately I decided to explore the relationship between journalists and subjects in football and it was far too close, far too incestuous and I kind of broke that if you like, and wrote about how the writers were telling the story the wrong way, how they were compromised by their relationship with the FAI and footballers. So I started off with a bang and this was a very firm conviction I held. Having been such an avid believer and reader of newspapers, I felt that really people who consume your newspaper, your radio programme, your television programme, are entitled to the real story, as raw as you can give it to them. So that conviction was born when I was a consumer of books and newspapers and television, so I went into it as an outsider. I went into it with a determination, which I hope I have to this day, to act in the interest of the person who is turning the dial or buying the paper.

RG: Well, one of those facets which you have, and it crops up again and again, is a sense of honesty. When one looks at RTÉ's standard of coverage of football, particularly the analysis, what do you believe makes RTÉ better than ITV or Sky?

ED: I think that the thing is to tell it as it is. We don't have close relationships with the people and we don't cultivate close relationships with the people we're analysing or commenting on, such as the Irish team or the Irish football manager. In England, it's much more incestuous. The media and the footballers and even television companies are all very close, they're all part of the same culture, they're all part of the same mob. It's like a mafia who kind of half do the job. In RTÉ they allow us to do the job un-compromisingly and people like Liam Brady and John Giles do it superbly. They have the knowledge and they're driven by what I think is a fine journalistic value — a desire to tell the public, who pay for the whole show, exactly what is going on and why it's happening or not happening and I think that's right. The public pay the piper.

RG: Is the public well served?

ED: They deserve to hear the tune. I don't think, in general, it is well enough served in all kinds of things, even this weekend and the G8 summit for example. Journalists are involved in hyp-ing things up. Journalists are involved in, basically, deceiving the public, not in a malicious way, but they get sucked into it. They're in the loop. The people are outside the loop and they decide what the people can have. Because if you tell it as it is, you are going to offend those who are powerful and who are close to you, who can do you favours, who can give you stories, who can give you an OBE or just their time to talk to you. So it's a rough old trade if you want to do it properly and you won't be very popular with your peers.

RG: Time and again on *Media Matters*, we talk about investigative journalism in terms of, I suppose, its demise rather than flourishing, which it should be doing. But what you are saying is that there's a cosy relationship between the PR people, the spin doctors and the journalists whereby, if you step outside the circle and expose unpalatable facets of a story or a politician for example, you will be in trouble and you won't get the interviews again. It is, therefore, controlled. Is that what you're saying?

ED: Yes, it is, and I must say that as someone who wrote opinion columns and did investigative journalism, I bow to investigative journalists — people like Frank Connolly. Frank is a very good example, someone whose stories and reportage have led to the creation of two tribunals, Morris and Flood, now Mahon. I bow to Frank and people like him. They are the really great journalists. People who rattle off opinions like me are a secondary breed and I don't put myself in the same category or league with the Frank Connollys of this world. But nevertheless, doing commentary and analysis, you can still do your best, do a good job.

RG: What provokes and what actually motivates you when you sit down to write an opinion piece?

ED: I'm anti-establishment. I don't like the ruling class. The ruling class in society . . .

RG: Do we have a ruling "class"?

ED: We have, yes, of course we have: the judiciary, the professions in this country. I don't like the ruling class in journalism. I don't like the powerful and the smug. I don't like those people. I identify more with the people on the street who are suffering generally. We see it every day from the behaviour, the collusion of powerful people in society. So it isn't an effort for me. It's not a stretch. I don't like the guys who run this show and I don't like the guys who run any show. So I'm a natural journalist. It's my vocation if you like.

RG: To be cynical and inquisitive?

ED: I'm not cynical in the least. If I was cynical I'd join the club and I'd probably be hanging out with these guys. I think journalists, at their best, are odd people. They're outsiders. They don't join clubs and they don't join gangs. They represent, basically, the ordinary person out there who doesn't have the information or access to the information that they need to understand how society works.

RG: But what you're saying, or what you said earlier, would contradict that because it means that journalists are not actually getting the stories in all instances.

ED: Yes, I mean there are cases around, the Frank McBrearty scandal in Donegal; the case of the Shell protestors. Five men from Mayo, who for five years couldn't make their voices heard, while this allegedly dangerous pipeline was going through their homes and their farms. So it's a struggle for people with causes to be heard in society and the journalists' obligation is to facilitate that wherever he or she can. And if you do that, then you won't be popular anywhere but you will, I think, get the respect of your audience who will say, "At least this journalist is trying to do it the best he can."

RG: Eamon, your relationship with John Giles had a bit of a blow during the 2002 World Cup and it seemed to drag on for about a year after that. How difficult was that and how did the reconciliation come about?

ED: Well it was difficult because we saw the Saipan controversy differently. But we both stuck to our guns as it were and hard things were said, principally by me I have to say. John's too much of a gentleman for that kind of stuff. We had a cool period but we've been friends for 40-odd years and after a few weeks of working together again, we forgot about it and we remain very good friends. John is a wonderful man. He's a gentleman really and a great analyst. He wouldn't have the kind of journalistic instincts that I have. He's in a different business of comment and analysis.

RG: I was going to say that he wouldn't actually classify himself as being a journalist, would he?

ED: He wouldn't. John is in a particular area of broadcasting. The rights and wrongs of it are for other people to decide. I felt very passionately about the Saipan incident. He felt passionately in another way. We differed, but you have to lay these things aside if you fundamentally get on with each other, which we have. It's over.

RG: That brings us neatly on to your relationship with Roy Keane which, of course, everyone will want to know about. When you were writing the biography, *Keane*, what was it like working with him because this nation, and I'm sure Great Britain as well, are fascinated by Roy Keane because of his individualism, because he stands outside the circle, to use that dreadful expression. So what is he like as a person?

ED: He's fascinating. We share a lot in common. I would like to flatter myself and say that he asked me to do the book. I wouldn't have ghosted an autobiography for anybody else, I can tell you. But he is fascinating, he is very intelligent, very passionate and is a driven sort of person and doesn't like establishments, to go back to something we spoke about earlier. He doesn't like the football establishment. He doesn't like what he calls the prawn sandwich brigade, the corporate guests at Old Trafford. He is a radical figure, he's interesting, he's passionate and I think his career has been outstanding and I suspect that he will have a big future as a coach and a manager in football. A thoroughly agreeable man, he's very funny, he's very witty, with a sardonic humour. In all, a terrific guy.

RG: And you reckon he's going to go on to football management, which is something you eschewed?

ED: I didn't. I tried to get a job, a number of jobs and I coached London University. I got my coaching qualifications but because I'd been an activist as a footballer in terms of rights for players and also I'd been a member of, among other parties, the Communist Party of Great Britain. I wasn't deemed to be officer material.

RG: At the time!

ED: At the time! I subsequently joined the PDs. I wasn't deemed to be officer material so in between I joined Fianna Fáil, Fine Gael and the Labour Party — so my politics are eclectic.

RG: Fair enough. Just coming back to your writing: *Four-Four-Two*, the well-respected football magazine, named three of your books in the top fifty football books of all time. Quite an accolade?

ED: I was astonished and thrilled because I've only written three books about football and that they were all there surprised me and I was thrilled with that — a very nice reflection on the books.

RG: Now to the U2 book, *The Unforgettable Fire*, which is obviously not about football! When you were working on that with them, what was the relationship between yourself, the band and indeed, Paul McGuinness?

ED: Well Paul McGuinness asked me to write the book. I didn't really want to write it because at the time I didn't feel I knew enough about music. In the end, after quite a long period of discussion and wooing, I agreed to do it. It wasn't a big money book at the time that he asked me to do it, because they weren't hugely known internationally, but I agreed to do it. I took two years to research it and I found them to be amazing, very professional. Bono is a very smart guy; Adam, a lovely guy; Edge is really talented; and there's a big organisation beside and behind them. Lots of Irish people. Joe O'Herlihy, their soundman, for example, is a hugely important factor in their success. McGuinness himself, as manager, is a great band manager and a cut above the spivs normally in that business. So they were fascinating and then I got very lucky because at the end of the two years of researching and writing, they made the front cover of *Time* magazine with the release of the *Joshua Tree* album. So my little book, which I hadn't got a deal for, became a book that everyone wanted to publish. I got lucky and made quite a lot of money and it was an interesting experience.

RG: "Made quite a lot of money" is obviously the phrase I'm going to pick up on there. In terms of your peers, do you find that there's a sense of jealousy . . . I'm thinking in terms of your relationship, whatever that might be, with Vincent Browne, which has been a fiery one for a long time.

ED: It has, yes. Well, I would say of Vincent Browne that he was the person who got me my first big break in journalism. He recommended me to John Mulcahy, when Mulcahy was starting the *Sunday Tribune* and I got the job as football correspondent and Vincent was extremely helpful to me at that point in my career.

RG: So what went wrong?

ED: Well, you know, I think there's a long list of people who've fallen out with Vincent. There isn't, in fact, a long list of people who've fallen out with me. The list in Vincent's case is enormous because of when he was publisher of the *Tribune* and *Magill*. He is mercurial. He is brilliant and continues to break great stories, as we've seen very recently in *Village* magazine, so I bear him no real ill will. Unfortunately, on his side of it, he continues to harbour whatever grudge he has. I think if I were to explain it and it's not for me to explain it, but sometimes, when you have been a patron of somebody, as he was to me, a big helper to me . . .

RG: . . . In the mentor sense?

ED: . . . Yes, the mentor sense; and then the thing that you've created turns out to have a mind of its own and will contradict you, I think that's difficult sometimes. Perhaps that's the reason why he continues to harbour what is an unimportant matter. I salute him as a journalist and indeed he's a very interesting man and I would love to have him on my radio programmes, but unfortunately we haven't been able to persuade him. But he's a great journalist.

RG: He is and I think he's also a great investigative journalist in the traditional sense. In fact he's very much in the same mould as yourself.

ED: I think he would be deeply offended by that observation, Roger. Because he would think that I'm just an upstart who really doesn't do the job. But certainly he has broken a lot of stories and he's a hugely important figure in Irish journalism and whatever he says about me won't alter certain facts.

RG: I want to move on now. You broke into radio journalism as a presenter of *The Last Word* on Today FM.

ED: And editor of that programme and indeed of the programme here on Newstalk 106, because I find it's important that one edits it as well as presents it.

RG: You have to have hands on control or . . .?

ED: Yes, you work with a team but the buck has to stop and the decisions have to be made about what's going to be in the programme. I was 51 when I started working for Radio Ireland, as it was then, and I was the most experienced person in the room. The tradition in broadcasting had been that the producer was the boss. Well, I wanted to change that and I think that the most experienced journalist should be the boss on programmes that are basically broadcast journalism. So editing the programmes that I present is important.

RG: Talk us through *The Last Word* and your experience there. It made a great inroad and certainly the listener figures were very high. Why did you leave?

ED: Well I had a good team and there were people who I felt weren't being paid as much as they should have been. There wasn't a career curve in Today FM, that's what concerned me most. We'd been doing the programme for five and a half years, which I think is a long time. One of the key people wasn't going to be rewarded as I felt he should have been. That was the principal reason. The other reason was to have a go at a talk show on television, which you'll no doubt gloss over very quickly.

RG: Unfortunately, we don't have time to go into that, so let's say it came and went!

ED: It lasted for 15 shows.

RG: Finally, your own show here on Newstalk 106, *The Breakfast Show*, how is that going do you think? Are you enjoying it?
And obviously, you've been recruited because of your status, because of your fame, so is it making the inroads that everyone
hopes it is?

ED: Well, the figures in radio in the JNLR system take about a
year to actually reflect reality. The first figure we got in February
showed that we have five times as many listeners as David
McWilliams had on the programme before. But we still carried
eight months of his figures. Now the figure we get in August will
be mostly for the work we've done since last September and the
full year book won't be out until next February. But I am enjoying
it. It's a terrific challenge. As you know, daily journalism is wherever you're doing it. I've no problem getting up in the mornings,
haven't missed a day, thank God, through ill-health or for any
other of the various reasons that arise and we are hopeful that in
August the figures will be encouraging for the radio station because it's a new station and new ventures in media always take
time and this station will go on and flourish and I hope that our
figures help in that process. We'll know in August how we're doing. But I'd be hopeful that we have an audience now and we've
established ourselves. The mornings are extremely competitive,
more competitive, much more competitive than the evening is, so
it's a big challenge. But life is invigorated by big challenges and I
think we'll be OK.

*Note: Eamon's predictions were right. In August 2005 the JNLRs returned a
listenership figure in the Dublin area of 24,000 for* The Breakfast Show.

*M*ichael *D*wyer

*M*any a film buff must envy the career path of Michael Dwyer who has had the good fortune of writing about film for over 25 years, for publications such as the Sunday Tribune, In Dublin *and* Screen International. *He's also presented programmes about film on RTÉ and for the past 16 years his insightful opinion and knowledge of film have graced the pages of* The Irish Times. *He also has the distinction of founding the Dublin Film Festival, twice, which perhaps says more about support for the arts in Ireland than it does about Michael Dwyer.*

RG: You grew up in Tralee and you were educated in St Brendan's, Killarney and Trinity College, Dublin. Did your passion for film originate in either of these two institutions?

MD: It began when I was very young in Tralee. I was still a very small schoolboy. My parents were avid cinema goers and there were three cinemas in Tralee at the time and they tended to go three nights a week. From when I was about four they started taking me with them to the seven o'clock shows. So I was seeing three movies with them every week and then on Saturdays I'd go to matinees with my school friends. I was seeing double bills then amounting to nine movies a week from the age of four or five.

RG: Any particular genre or just whatever hit Tralee?

MD: Absolutely everything and I became addicted at a very young age.

RG: And what sort of influences do you think crept in at that age in terms of the type of film that you ended up either enjoying or disliking?

MD: I liked everything. Obviously we were restricted to almost entirely American movies and some British films because that was the nature of commercial cinemas in an Irish town at the time. I knew how addicted I'd become when I spent my last three years of secondary school, in a boarding school, where we were restricted to one movie a month as chosen by the priest.

RG: One movie a month! What was it, *The Nun's Story* over and over again?

MD: Yes, or similar things, so I suffered severe withdrawal symptoms, but every holidays I'd have to come up to Dublin for a long weekend and go and see maybe nine movies, just to catch up.

RG: Well to go from a veritable feast of movies to that kind of starvation must have been quite a blow particularly given the frequency with which you had been going. Did your critical faculties click in at that stage as to what was good and what was bad?

MD: Absolutely. I remember one of the first films that really struck me as more than just another movie, but as something extraordinarily special, was *Bonnie and Clyde*, Arthur Penn's great film with Warren Beatty and Faye Dunaway. It was on in Tralee for a week and I went three nights out of the six and stayed for the two shows on the last night. It changed my view of film radically, probably because it was so different in the way it dealt with violence on film, the way it dealt with these two characters and the myths created around them. The sheer style of it and the astonishing final sequence where they're killed in slow motion, opened my eyes to cinema in a very different way.

RG: Well, in fact you say that that is your favourite film, is it your favourite film still?

MD: That's a question I get asked fairly often as you'd expect in this job and yes, it is. I mean there are many others, very many others.

RG: But just staying with *Bonnie and Clyde* for a while, if my maths is right, you'd have been in your mid teens at that stage when it came out.

MD: I was underage of course! It was over-18s, but I was tall for my age.

RG: There were all kinds of adventurous things in that movie, including the first reference, certainly that I can recall, to oral sex.

MD: Yes indeed. It was a film well ahead of its time. It was interesting that Warren Beatty was only 30 when he produced it and did it against all the odds. Warners had no confidence in it so they gave him a great big back-end deal so he got a huge portion of the profits from the film. It went through several directors. Even

Truffaut was supposed to direct it at one stage before Arthur Penn was taken on board to do it and he did such a brilliant job.

RG: As you say, the violence in it, particularly the end, the slow motion killing, was something that I'd never seen before. The horror of it was absolutely harrowing, which you don't actually see now in films; they tend to go over the top in terms of the blood and gore.

MD: Oh absolutely. I think people have probably become more desensitised since. I mean the film played with the way they'd rob the bank and they'd head off in their jalopy to this jaunty, hillbilly music by Flatt and Scruggs. Then suddenly there's a scene where a member of the bank staff runs out, they shoot him in the face and the blood rolls all over his glasses. It wipes the smiles off everybody's faces.

RG: Indeed; and moving on from the influences of *Bonnie and Clyde* and presumably a lot of others as well, you came to Dublin to Trinity College. When you left Trinity did you at that stage decide that you wanted to be in film in one guise or another or had you made your mind up that you wanted to be in journalism?

MD: Not at all, I didn't really know what I wanted to do, so I went back to Tralee and worked for a few years in the county library, which gives you a very orderly approach to everything with things like the discipline of cataloguing.

RG: Well, yes, I suppose systems would be high on their list.

MD: Yes, it does give you a very orderly mind. But there was a film society in Tralee showing foreign films at the time and the same people had been running it for about ten years and were getting a bit tired of it. I was young and full of energy. I threw myself into it and expanded it to the point where we took over an old cinema, one of the ones I used to go to as a kid. It had 620 seats. We managed to fill it every second Monday night for the whole period of October through to the end of March.

RG: And what kind of material were you putting on? Presumably you were choosing them?

MD: I was choosing them all, everything, Pasolini, Fassbinder, classics, we showed Hitchcock's *Blackmail* in a silent version with no sound whatsoever, no piano accompaniment. We really got the crowds. People were travelling from all over to come to the film society and it was a great way of unleashing my passion. I really enjoyed it enormously and it led me to going into work fulltime in film. The film society movement was really growing then, in the late seventies, and the Arts Council funded a full-time appointment in Dublin to co-ordinate all the film society activities in the country. I applied and I got the job.

RG: But getting audiences in Tralee for the likes of Fassbinder was not a problem, quite clearly, so tastes were quite advanced?

MD: To be fair we used a few lures. Quite a few very good movies were banned at the time. I remember films like *Carnal Knowledge* and those, so we'd show them because we were exempt from censorship as a private club. So people who were looking for a bit of titillation had to work their way through a lot of Kurosawa and very serious cinema as well.

RG: Well at that stage was *The Kerryman* (the paper as opposed to the being), objecting to some of the films that were on?

MD: On the contrary, they were hugely supportive. Tony Meade, the deputy editor and Seamus McConville, the editor, gave us loads of space every year when the season was announced and they were extremely supportive, as was the other local paper, *Kerry's Eye*.

RG: Moving on to your own career in journalism, what drew you to writing? You started with *In Dublin*, am I right?

MD: I was running the Film Society office in Dublin and a friend of mine had asked me on a radio show, on a pirate radio station at the time, to talk about it and he said, "We could do with someone to talk about movies once a week if you're interested." So I started doing things for a station called Big D Radio which had people like Dave Fanning, Mark Storey and Gerry Ryan . There was an *In Dublin* radio show presented by Gerry Ryan. I started doing some stuff on that and then the magazine *In Dublin* asked me if I would sit in for their critic while he was away. Then when he came back they said that they could do with the two of us. I remember my first review was most inauspicious — it was *International Velvet* with Tatum O'Neill.

RG: Oh dear oh dear!

MD: But it got better.

RG: And I don't suppose your review for that was in the least bit flattering, or was it?

MD: No, but I spent hours writing it, getting every comma and dot right!

RG: From *In Dublin*, then, you moved to the *Sunday Tribune*.

MD: That's right. *In Dublin* was a great place at the time. John Doyle was the editor, Colm Tóibín was the features editor.

RG: People like Fintan O'Toole were there.

MD: Yes, in fact it's funny so many of the people who were there are now all in *The Irish Times*: Fintan O'Toole doing theatre; Michael Dervan doing classical music; Aidan Dunne doing visual arts; me doing film. We are all in the same place again. In 1983 when Vincent Browne set up the *Sunday Tribune*, which had failed once, he took Fintan and myself and several other people over from In Dublin into the *Tribune* and it was very exciting to work for a national newspaper for the first time.

RG: So at that stage you were an established critic with a national newspaper, albeit it a Sunday newspaper, and did you realise that that was where you wanted to be?

MD: I was loving it! I had really loved the whole *In Dublin* experience. There was a small group of us there who wrote a lot for *In Dublin* and quite often — the magazine was published on Thursdays and it usually arrived in from the printers on Wednesday evenings — we'd all congregate down in the office and go off and have a pint and have a look at it. There was a great charge of energy and excitement about the whole place at the time. I knew this was what I wanted to do — finally!

RG: While you were working for the *Sunday Tribune*, you then turned around and did what you'd done down in Tralee many years before, and start another film festival, in this case the Dublin Film Festival. Tell me about that.

MD: It's hard to believe now because there's such a proliferation of film festivals all over the country. But at that time there was only one film festival and that was the long-established festival in Cork. Dublin has always had a great cinema-going audience and the figures are still the highest per capita of any European city.

RG: And that's been with us a good while now.

MD: It has been. It's been a great tradition that goes right back to when people used to book to go to the cinemas on Sunday night and buy tickets from touts outside to get in.

RG: That's right, I remember the queues outside the cinemas in O'Connell Street.

MD: Except nowadays they book online. However, Myles Dungan and I used to do a lot of radio together and we came up with the idea of starting a Dublin Film Festival and launched it in the autumn of 1985. It was very successful. I programmed it for the first six years and we had lots and lots of interesting guests in for retrospectives and for the Festival itself.

RG: And you had a lot of heavyweights. I can remember Oliver Stone, for one, when you got him to come over with *JFK*.

MD: That's right, except that was the year after I finished although I did do the public interview with Oliver Stone on stage in the Abbey which was something else. We'd people like Paul Schrader, Margarethe von Trotta, Ken Russell, who was quite a handful as you'd expect, quite a prima donna, and a whole lot of emerging people as well. It was great and it grew and grew.

RG: And it vanished in 1997 was it?

MD: No it lasted until about 2000 or 2001 when it just stopped. And as it happened, two years ago, a few of us who'd been involved at various stages in the old Festival, decided to re-start it. I suppose the only difference being that this one has a different name, it's the Dublin International Film Festival because, for various reasons, we needed to distinguish it from the other one.

RG: So between that and the day job with *The Irish Times* you must be very busy. You also tour the world to attend film festivals. It sounds terribly glamorous, but people who haven't attended the Cannes Film Festival imagine all kinds of wonderful things, but in point of view Cannes is a chore, is it not?

MD: It's really hard work. I mean you phone the office and they ask, "What's the weather like?" And I say, "As I moved from one cinema to another this morning after my half eight press show and went on to my eleven o'clock show, it was nice for the two minutes I saw it." I think the only people who don't work in Cannes are the people who come back with suntans and they are very, very few people. It's a really intensive twelve days and it doesn't matter if it's a Saturday or a Sunday it's round the clock from eight in the morning 'til very late at night. Some years it can be great and other years it can be terrible if the selection of films is erratic. There have been a few really bad years and most of them recently.

RG: There are heavy demands on press people and the pressures to go to this show or that show is always severe and you're at it, as you say, from half eight in the morning until midnight and presumably you've meetings in between.

MD: Absolutely, and this year for example when the *Fahrenheit 9/11* show came to town, it just took over the Festival for a day. All I could do for that day was to concentrate on that film. See it in the morning, write it up, go to Michael Moore's very long but very useful press conference, then go and write it up and that was most of the day gone just on one film, but obviously a very important film which did win the Palme d'Or.

RG: You've been going there for 23 years, so you've seen it grow. But more importantly you've seen the Irish involvement in Cannes grow from the mid-eighties — I can remember being there then with *Eat the Peach* as you recall and many things since — but really Ireland's presence has increased for such a small country in the world market place.

MD: Yes, the first year I went was in 1982 when they were still building the new Palais. *ET* was the closing film and there were only two other Irish people there, Seamus Smith and Ray Co-miskey, who was the film critic with *The Irish Times* at the time — just the three of us. Now there's about 200 Irish delegates registered at the Irish pavilion. There is an Irish pavilion on the Crois-sette now and there has been for a number of years, so the Irish influence has absolutely grown. Although there were the seeds of it that very first year I was there because *Angel*, Neil Jordan's first film, was shown in the market and became a very big hit. It was just shown in a few back street cinemas but the word spread and a lot of internationally important critics and distributors were willing to stand during it just so they could see it and it really caught on. It just shows what Cannes can do for a film.

RG: Well we know that the Irish film industry is growing but whether it's making any inroads in terms of distribution is another problem, isn't it?

MD: It is indeed. But it's overcome one obstacle and that is finding an audience on home turf. It's great to see Irish movies speaking to Irish audiences but quite often films that do really well here just don't work at all abroad. I suppose the most classic example being *Veronica Guerin*, which was the biggest hit of the year here a year ago and did virtually nothing anywhere else.

RG: Sure, well I can think of many, for example *When Brendan Met Trudy* did well here, *About Adam* did well also but they didn't seem to translate to an international audience. But, of course you get into a contentious area defining the nationality of a film which is always very difficult. When you take films like *The Crying Game* or even *My Left Foot* which in both cases are Irish stories with Irish directors and Irish writers but not necessarily Irish films because of the way they are financed.

MD: Well I suppose there's British finance in both films but the directors are Irish and virtually the entire cast and crew of *My Left Foot* was Irish and both films were rejected by Cannes as a matter of interest. They are two of the great Irish films. But at the same time you look at a lot of the biggest hits in France, or Italy or Germany every year which are usually police thrillers or comedies that rarely ever travel. Comedy in particular is the most difficult thing to travel beyond borders and even a lot of big American hit comedies don't really work over here because they're too localised in terms of references.

RG: This applies to American films and, I suppose to a degree British ones that can transcend borders in terms of the sense of humour and are more universal or more readily accepted elsewhere.

MD: Yes, but even *Four Weddings and a Funeral*, a definitively British film, was released in America first and became a hit and then they released in Britain as America's number one hit comedy!

RG: Over the years, do you think the film industry worldwide, in terms of standards of films from a critical point of view, have improved or not?

MD: I think cinema always goes through cycles and we're probably not going through a vintage period at the moment. I think the cinema of the sixties and the seventies was outstanding. There was some great work in America. It's probably the last period when great films were being made without test previews. Now everything is compromise and is tested down to the last line. Anything that doesn't work with the test audience in Virginia or

Kansas or wherever is taken out because it's felt it wouldn't appeal to the audience. Whereas you had that period in the sixties and the seventies when people like Scorsese and Francis Coppola and Brian de Palma, Alan Pakula, were all at their best and most uncompromising. I mean most of them have done much inferior work since. It was a great period in Europe as well where you had Truffaut, Godard, Rohmer, Pasolini, Fellini and De Sica, it was a great time. I can't think of too many comparable directors today. I suppose, on the other hand, sometimes films really only show their endurance after a period of time, when they've had time to settle and when they take on a greater importance ten years later. It's often the case.

Carol Flynn

*T*he interviewees in Under the Spotlight *are predominantly journalists and broadcasters. However, we endeavour to include as broad a range of people as we can by drawing on the many different disciplines of media practice. One such category is that of public relations practitioners who work with journalists on a regular basis, albeit in a somewhat strained companionship. Carol Flynn worked as a journalist on provincial newspapers, with the Irish Press Group and, when it ceased operations, with Independent Newspapers. Some years ago Carol Flynn made the switch from journalism to public relations, a career change frequently undertaken by journalists. Clearly Carol has made a success of her PR career and is Managing Director of McConnells Public Relations, one of the leading PR consultancies in the country. At the time of her interview on* Media Matters, *Carol had just been elected Chairperson of the Public Relations Consultants Association, the*

representative body of the PR profession. Journalism is in Carol's blood. Her father, Liam Flynn, was a well-known figure in Irish journalism and had been both news editor and, more latterly, art (photographic) editor of the Irish Press Group. I was intrigued to know what had made her switch career from journalism to public relations.

RG: First of all, Carol, you, like many in public relations, were a journalist in your past life. So what brought you into journalism?

CF: Well I suppose I grew up in a media family. My father was a journalist. He'd been news editor in the Press Group and became art editor. My life, from when I was out of the cradle, was literally knowing about the news stories of the day and the exciting things that were happening. It really captivated my imagination and all the way along I don't think there was anything else I ever wanted to be but a journalist.

RG: So you wanted to be a journalist by dint of the fact that your father was, and you lived journalism on a daily basis as you were growing up, was that it?

CF: Around the dinner table every evening, he would tell us the stories of the day, what exciting things had happened, the challenges and how he had to deal with them. As a child I remember the phone ringing late at night. For instance when the Stardust disaster struck — a tragic story — I remember being woken up by constant phone calls and different things happening all night. I lived through the story as it emerged through the night and the whole family got up to find out what was happening. I remember too the oil tanker that went down off Cork and again that was a phenomenal story that happened through the night. It was a question of trying to get planes and helicopters to get photographers to go down there and get on board and get the pictures and the story back in time for the newspaper the following day. As you can imagine, as a child, this was all terribly exciting.

When famous figures came into town the journalists had a ring-side seat at every event and I thought, "This must be a wonderful job. You can meet film stars, rock stars, whatever you want. You can have an eye on the world that lots of other careers won't give you." So all along I just aimed to be a journalist.

RG: When you say you aimed to be a journalist, what course did you take? Did you go in as a copy girl in the traditional sense or did you do a degree first or what?

CF: I studied journalism in Rathmines and on completing that I went to Cork to do a course in radio which the government had set up prior to legalising local radio. Then I went to work with the *Clare Champion* and spent a bit of time there learning about local government and the local court process.

RG: So you were covering courts and councils, the time-honoured torture!

CF: Yes, and I did the basic things and I found them fascinating. I thought it was the most exciting time to be part of something really interesting that was happening on a daily basis. And of course every story seems to be so important and you feel you're part of it. I came back to Dublin and I freelanced with practically all of the newspapers around town and did some work in RTÉ on a couple of radio programmes there. Then I ended up as a staff reporter in the Irish Press Group.

RG: So were you on general reporting as part of the news team there?

CF: Yes, I was part of the news team and worked across all of the different titles, the *Sunday*, the *Irish* and *Evening Press* and I had great experiences there. Obviously being the city slicker and despite the fact that I'd spent some time in Clare with the *Champion* and some time in Cork, my news editor said at one point, "I think we really need to send you around the country because you need to know a bit more about what is happening out there." And it was the most wonderful experience. I was sent off on a jaunt for two months all around the country, writing stories about travel, about holiday homes, about local government — whatever struck me.

RG: So you had broad experience in journalism. Were you with the Press Group up to the time of its demise?

CF: I was there 'til the bitter end and like all my colleagues lamented the fact that we were to close. During that period I'd obviously covered all the key stories of the day and worked on a number of really, really exciting challenges. So we were all very, very sad to see it go.

RG: There were a lot of journalists out on the street at that time because there wasn't that much employment around. There was a lot of spare capacity but not enough jobs.

CF: No, there were very few jobs at that time and there were two hundred journalists on the street.

RG: Was that the reason you went into public relations?

CF: It certainly was. It wasn't something I'd considered, it wasn't an area I had looked at. Many other journalists and colleagues of mine did the same thing subsequently. The *Irish Press* staff had gone on strike. No one was receiving any payment and I ran a big event and invited all the public relations companies in Dublin to put their money where there mouth is and finally support the people that had supported them for so long, which they all duly did. We organised a huge event and everybody turned up. At that point, I was recognised by Bill O'Herlihy who approached me and asked me would I work with him.

RG: Ah, so you were head-hunted by Bill O'Herlihy. And what was that transition like? Because some cruel people have suggested the difference between journalism and public relations is the same as the difference between prostitution and pimping! But of course I wouldn't suggest that in your case! So what did it feel like, going from being the game keeper to the poacher — or should that be vice versa?

CF: Well at the same time, I was very lucky because the *Irish Independent* also asked me to work for them on their features pages. It was a tough call because both options were exciting and I spoke with Bill and said, "I'll think about it", and went on to work for the *Irish Independent* for a year after the *Press* closed, writing two or three features a week for them. It was another great experience and then Bill O'Herlihy came back to me. He'd kept in touch throughout the course of that year and as projects came up that he was dealing with and which he thought would be suitable for me to work on, he made contact. When I finally decided to move to the other side it was working with a number of government ministers, advising them on strategy and media management.

RG: And this would have been of the Fine Gael persuasion, presumably?

CF: Fine Gael and Labour was the government in power at the time. Some of the projects there were extremely interesting and I thought, "Well, why not? I'll give it a shot, it won't rule out my journalism days forever and it's something different." I also think that one of the interesting things about changing career is that we've got to remember no job is for life anymore and that really is true, no matter what you do or where. You've got to be open-minded and I think at the end of the day, when there's a closure, people become terrified and they become paralysed for a time about what they're going to do. They ask, "Will I ever work again?" On the day we heard that the *Press* was closing down, I remember thinking that I was only in my twenties and feeling, "Will I ever work again?" But of course everyone does and everyone has gone on to do significant other things and I think you've got to be quite open minded and you've got to learn something new.

RG: But did you find it difficult? The standard rule of journalism is of course to endeavour to be objective but when you're in public relations you're representing one side, the same as a lawyer would be. Did you find that shift of emphasis problematic?

CF: No, not at all. I think one of the key things in public relations that you've got to remember is to be truthful. You're there to deliver a message as precisely as you properly can. It's not about telling untruths. If you're true to yourself from that perspective you can do your job properly.

RG: Yes, but whereas you mightn't be putting forward an untruth or a direct lie as a PR person, you mightn't be emphasising a negative aspect of it, to put it politely. So, in other words, one aspect of the story mightn't come to the surface.

CF: Well, obviously in PR your job is to present your client in the best light possible and that's essentially what you're being paid to do. As a former journalist as well, you understand what the media want. You understand what will make a story and so at the end of the day you know the key points that they need to be able to put a story together.

RG: Well yes, that indeed is a very important point and it was one that I made in the introduction in emphasising the fact that you were a journalist. But would you go along with the accusation that there aren't enough journalists in PR, or former journalists in PR, and that what has happened is that a whole sort of breed of people have grown up and been trained as PR consultants without having any real understanding of how the media works.

CF: That charge could be made against both sides: on the one hand, the media not understanding the business environment and on the other, the PR person not understanding the media environment. I think it does help having been a former journalist but having said that, there's lots of areas of PR that are not about media management. A lot of the very large agencies would say that maybe only 40 per cent of their business is about talking to the media. The rest is about advising clients in terms of business-to-business relationships, in terms of developing programmes or marketing campaigns, that don't necessarily involve the media.

RG: Yes, but very often and certainly in my experience, the client wants his or her product on the front page of *The Irish Times* every day if possible. I exaggerate, of course, but that tends to be the demand of the client and saying that 40 to 45 per cent of the work is purely media relations would seem very low to me.

CF: Well, I think at the end of the day many clients, particularly if you're dealing with the marketing side, will look at different campaigns. It may be promoting a health campaign but they'll promote it through retail or by talking to customers on the street. There's lots of new communications methods out there now; it might be on the internet; it may be sending out posters; recruiting people in different ways. There's a much more complex landscape and quite a sophisticated media relationship landscape out there now and more than just the newspapers.

RG: What I want to get on to talking about now is the PR industry and its image. Does PR, ironically, need a bit of PR?

CF: Well I think at the end of the day the difficulty with PR is you are delivering messages and people can then interpret that as being "fed a line". Because of that there's always a sense that as the relationships with journalists and the media are very, very close, there are always a number of instances that raise people's eyebrows. But I think it's the same for any industry. The PR industry is growing in Ireland and it's quite a sophisticated machine. The numbers of people going into it are growing and the number of companies that are using it are growing. I believe that that's testament to the fact that it's working and that people do actually believe in it. But as a result as well, it's being challenged a lot more and it's under the spotlight a lot more.

RG: I want to come back to government PR in a minute but I want to get your views on what we hear from news editors. Some have told us on this programme that they're plagued by PR people, at four or half four on a daily basis, ringing up to ask if you're coming to this or that reception which, when it comes down to it, they've already judged, they've seen the invitation and they know that in nine out of ten cases there's not a story in it. When you were a journalist you must have undergone some of that but now you're in that situation of trying to persuade, coerce, cajole media people along to press receptions which they don't really want to go to.

CF: Absolutely! I mean at the end of the day that is part of the game between the two sides. If you don't follow up with a phone call to ask did they receive the invitation — they may not have, it may have been thrown in the bin or it may not have arrived there — there's no one more irate than a journalist who didn't receive an invitation who had expected one.

RG: In fairness, that is true.

CF: There really is a necessity to follow it up with a phone call and I appreciate, again, the number of phone calls they may be getting. Perhaps it's a job for the newspapers to put someone in place to receive those phone calls and process them from an admin perspective. In terms of creating relationships with journalists, well that's another side of the game where you will talk to individual journalists and develop a relationship with them on behalf of a client.

RG: Sure, but you Carol, worked in journalism for a long time so you know what the inside of a newspaper office looks like, or indeed a radio station. The concern is that those people who are working in PR who have perhaps only spent a week on work experience on a local newspaper, have no idea of the pressures that press people are under. Is that not the case?

CF: I'm sure it can be but at the end of the day everyone has to learn somewhere as well. You've got to start developing your media relationships at some point in your career. Ideally they would follow a seasoned operator for some period of time and then understand how the system works but in a realistic world that's not how it happens.

RG: You were talking of government PR and you have worked in that area yourself as you've said. Only two weeks ago the *Sunday Tribune* broke the story that €20 million was being expended, not all on PR but a good percentage thereof, when there are plenty of good press officers in government departments. Can you explain that one, not just to me but for the listeners, because I'm sure there's a lot of curiosity out there as to why, on top of paid press officers in the departments, every minister needs to have their own PR person.

CF: Well I think to be honest the demands of those in government requires availability and to have responses immediately — the fact that we're working in an immediate society — when a story happens it happens. There's no time to go and research your material, to find your back-up and your support system. At the end of the day that is a realistic issue for everybody in every area of business now — that you're expected to respond efficiently and immediately. I think that that has led to the increase in the number of PR people. The other thing is that while there may be press officers in the department, their role may be defined in a different way. I'm sure different departments have different systems but their role will be defined: to issue the releases on the day, to maybe follow the minister, to follow the diary and to liaise with the media. But there may be bigger things that are happening or other things that are happening that they can't deal with along with that and that's when they will employ another PR agency.

RG: What you've implied is that it's basically a response that's driving the need for extra PR people. A lot of people, the cynics amongst us and the journalists amongst us, say that spin is also there and it's not just with the government because Alastair Campbell took it to a fine art and more before him and we have the same type of beast in this country. So people will say that it's not just a response, it's not just getting the answer out, it's getting the right one out, the one that's going to create the least damage.

CF: Well at the end of the day it is a requirement of everyone to get their message out there and the message that they believe in. I suppose everyone employs different tactics and different tools to do that and, as I say again, the increased media attention and demand for instant, efficient responses to whatever query it may be necessitates, quite a big machine.

RG: Now, in a word or two, can you tell us about the role of the Public Relations Consultants Association?

CF: Well, essentially it represents the industry, members of the industry and helps to try and regulate how they perform, it sets standards and criteria called Consultancy Management Standards to which each member must subscribe to be practitioners and members of the Association.

RG: Right; so what it presumably does as well is look after conduct, behaviour, ethics — which is a ridiculous word in both journalism and public relations, but it's bandied around a lot so I feel the need to mention it. So you look after that as well in the PRCA, is that right?

CF: We do.

RG: Moving on to another topic — and it's not necessarily off the topic of ethics — but the situation that incensed a lot of people over the last while was the Martin Cullen / Monica Leech situation. What would your views be on that in terms of the amount of money she, ostensibly, was receiving for PR advice?

CF: I don't want to refer to any specific cases, obviously, but I think when it comes to the money for PR campaigns, what is often presented when we read in the newspapers about the amounts spent on PR is the total campaign that is being implemented. It may include the cost of posters, it may include the cost of an event, it may include video input, it can include a lot of things other than PR fees. The fees in the industry are fairly standard across most agencies. You can obviously never know the numbers, as it varies from agency to agency and project to project, or the experience of an individual working on the campaign.

RG: But in this instance, it was a retainer fee, a consultancy fee. I don't think it actually had any third-party costs in it, or did it?

CF: I think there were some third-party costs there. But in terms of the fees, I mean obviously it did put the spotlight on the PR industry. Again, without knowing the detail of what she was required to do in terms of the campaign, it's very hard to judge. The one difficulty the public relations profession has had is in terms of people seeing them as a professional body. If you go to a solicitor or if you go to an accountant, you expect to pay fees by the hour. You expect to pay certain rates and people don't have a problem doing that.

RG: Yes, but solicitors are a lot more established whereas PR is, relatively speaking, a new profession and therefore people aren't *au fait* with it. You mentioned fees and one of the things that a lot of people have criticism for is how the PR industry itself is abused by clients, or would-be clients, looking to tender four or five different agencies, get their good ideas, on which the PR firm has spent hours, without any fees for the work. What's your view on that?

CF: It's very, very difficult for the industry. The amount of time spent on preparing presentations, putting them together, putting vast amounts of an individual's hours into it, plus maybe third-party costs in preparing surveys or questionnaires or videos to make your presentation, can cost quite a lot of money. One agency estimated it cost them €28,000 to put a presentation together for a government department and they didn't win. It's a huge cost to pitch. I don't think a lot of people really understand that, in trying to be fair by inviting a number of agencies to participate.

RG: I think there's an awful lot of commercial companies who know exactly what they're doing in that instance and they're just getting as many ideas as they can from as many PR companies and then they go off and do it themselves.

CF: It can happen but I think people who try and do it themselves will discover that that's where the expertise lies.

*N*óirín *H*egarty

*S*tudying journalism in the College of Commerce in Rathmines in Dublin has been the starting point for many successful journalists in this country. For the graduates of this course, a spell on a provincial newspaper usually follows. Such was the career route for Nóirín Hegarty who, having completed the course in Rathmines, worked on the Tullamore Tribune *before freelancing for the Irish Press Group and then moving to* The Irish Times. *After three years there she went to work in journalism in Australia. When she returned from her travels, she worked for the Independent Newspaper Group and became Deputy Editor of the* Evening Herald *for a period of seven years. At the time of this interview, Nóirín Hegarty had just been appointed editor of the* Sunday Tribune *and thus became the second woman in this country to be appointed editor of a national newspaper.*

RG: Has the appointment been a big change for you?

NH: Well it's a very different pace of life working for a daily newspaper, an evening newspaper, where the news agenda changes sometimes by the minute and certainly by the hour. From the news conference at 6.00 in the morning it can be a completely different ball game by 8.00. So the pace is very different on a Sunday newspaper, but it does provide the opportunity to look at stories in more detail and to do some more investigative journalism. I've also learned, from very early on, the perils of Sunday journalism which is when the potential splash for a Sunday is run in a Saturday newspaper and you're left then trying to find something.

RG: I can imagine. Going back to the *Herald* though; you were issuing at least two editions a day, if not more?

NH: Well three editions a day, the early edition which would go to the country mainly and be in Dublin for the lunchtime trade and then a racing edition because the racing declarations would be important when they come in from PA at about 11.30. Then a final edition which would be updated with all the courts and the various happenings of the morning.

RG: It's interesting that you mention racing because that is an essential ingredient of an evening paper, isn't it? By that I mean people tend to get it, not so much for its news content, but more for either the television or sport.

NH: Absolutely. You remove things like that from an evening newspaper at your peril. Also things like courts and sports; but you could make the same analogy with a provincial newspaper. People expect to have certain things in the paper and your job is to make sure that they are there and they're up to date with whatever's happening. But your greatest demand is that you meet the deadline. Whereas with a Sunday newspaper it's a very different demand because you're offering something unique and something different.

RG: Well what exactly are you offering when it comes down to it on a Sunday? For the most part it tends to be comment and analysis of the week's news doesn't it?

NH: To a certain extent, but I think there certainly is room in the market for good investigative journalism, for breaking news stories and I would see that as being a primary objective. Then secondly to provide an alternative view on what has happened in the week or to give some extra information or to take a different perspective or to provide some quality writing by particular writers who introduce you to different individuals or their views on what has happened. It's an opportunity to bring the rolling news stories of the week to another level. You've got to offer something more. There's got to be a compelling reason to read a paper on a Sunday. People are busy. I have this age-old argument about people being time poor. It's not just the quality of the journalism you're offering, it's the second it takes a person to look at the pictures, to look at the headline and to make that split second judgement: "Will I bother reading on or won't I?"

RG: That's precisely it and the other thing is that many people, and certainly I would get three or four Sundays and by the time I'm finished in here I carry a guilt complex for the whole week that I haven't read every single supplement, be it in *The Observer*, the *Times* or the *Tribune*.

NH: I think you've got to be aware of your market. We're very fortunate in the *Tribune*, and I feel very fortunate that I've come into a very talented team of journalists, but we also have a very loyal readership and I would mess with that readership at my peril. You know, it's not a case of dumbing down the paper, it's

not a case of bringing the paper more upmarket, it's a case of providing that diversity, the stories that reflect people's lives and
their experiences, the stories that inform them, the stories that entertain them to a certain extent as well. Also to provide opinion
from recognised commentators from viewpoints that people
would be interested in reading.

RG: You mentioned investigative journalism; for the most part
over the last few years there's been a shortage of investigative
journalism in this country and, indeed, in the UK. When it comes
down to it there's been nothing like the Insight team in *The Sunday
Times*, going back to the Harold Evans days in that paper. Can we
afford it any more?

NH: It's hugely expensive to do good investigative journalism
but the alternative is, you don't do it at all. So then what do you
do? Do you buy into the cult of the celebrity? That's where you're
going to reflect on what happens on the television! I think you've
got to try and set the agenda to some extent and certainly from
my perspective as an editor, I would see that it's an area worthy
of resources. It's an area worth exploring further, putting good
people into that area and giving them the opportunity to get under the skin of stories and to break stories. Not just offering a perspective on rolling stories. It's very important that we break stories. It's not rocket science. What sells newspapers is good stories
and good pictures and that's what we need to be about. I think the
reader is very discerning and expects a certain standard in the rest
of the paper, expects good sports coverage, expects a decent
magazine, expects good business coverage. But ultimately they're
buying newspapers for news coverage.

RG: You're at the top of your profession and you're the second
woman ever to be appointed editor of a national newspaper in
this country. How did it all begin for you?

NH: I went a well-worn route, the College of Commerce in Rathmines. But I suppose if you go right back, and I was thinking of this as I was coming to talk to you today, the first thing I ever had published was in a magazine in London called *Ginty* when I was nine and that's where my interest comes from. My family are from the west of Ireland, from west Clare. I have an uncle in Milltown Malbay, Martin Bowen, and I remember as a very young child there would be storms off the west coast and he would go, the morning after a bad storm, to see if bodies had been washed up from wrecks of ships and that sort of thing and I just thought this was an amazing thing to do. It was purely curiosity at that stage and there was no humane virtue involved in it. And I do remember then another very important incident which was the Tiede Herrema kidnapping. He was held in Monasterevin for three weeks and again due to my west of Ireland connection, we were travelling up and down to Clare at the time and I thought "this is really happening" when we were passing through Monasterevin and it certainly developed my interest from then on. I went to the College of Commerce in Rathmines after school and I did what was in those days, a Certificate in Journalism. There wasn't a variety of courses in the early eighties.

RG: It's only relatively recently that more have come on stream.

NH: I think at that stage there may have been a postgraduate course in NIHE as it was.

RG: Now DCU.

NH: That's right and when I left college I went to the *Tullamore Tribune* to work, which was a fantastic start because there was a 10,000 readership. If you made mistakes, they'd tell you about it on the street. Or you'd be offered a fiver to keep a name out of the paper. So it was very much in your face and it was a fantastic learning experience.

RG: Did you get a lot of that on the *Tullamore Tribune*, of fivers being offered?

NH: I wouldn't say a lot of it, but yes, absolutely, it did happen in those days. Remember, we're going back to the mid-eighties and I'm sure the environment has changed now and it's probably a lot more sophisticated. But yes, in a small environment, courts were the mainstay of the newspaper. If someone was in court for drink driving or for a variety of other offences, the last thing they wanted was their name in the paper. But I should say we ran them all, to set the record straight!

RG: You were never corrupted!

NH: There was an editor called Geoff Oakley at the time and Seamus Dooley, whom you know, was a reporter there and it was a very honourable environment and a great training ground, I must say.

RG: Where did you go from there?

NH: I came back to Dublin after that and I worked in a free-lance capacity for the Press Group and then I worked for *The Irish Times* for three years covering courts, which again is a fantastic way for a young journalist to start out because it demands absolute accuracy.

RG: So in the old style, you have shorthand then, presumably, from the two years in the College?

NH: Absolutely, because I went to Rathmines in an era when there was a very famous shorthand teacher who has since passed away, Mairéad Doyle, and by God you learned your shorthand and you made sure that you got there and passed the exams. She was a very strict task mistress.

RG: And of course shorthand is something that's not encouraged anymore, really, in the courses.

NH: Well there are so many other ways to take a note nowadays that it isn't as vital any more.

RG: You then moved from the *Times* to the *Herald*, was it?

NH: No, I actually went to Australia after that and I worked as a business reporter, which wasn't my background in Ireland. It's very difficult to go into a new world as it was, without contacts as a reporter. I didn't have sub-editing skills at the time, so I got work as a business journalist because it was easier to build up my contacts book on the ground. So I worked for the *Sydney Morning Herald*, more in an analysis-type capacity writing in the features department. And then I worked for *Pacific Computer Weekly* which is a business publication serving the Asian-Pacific rim and then came back to Ireland and I worked for Independent Newspapers.

RG: And moved into the *Herald*, or were you on the *Independent*?

NH: I was on the *Independent* first as a general reporter. In fact I came back to Ireland, this was in the late eighties, with the intention of going on to Canada within three months and I said if I got a job offer within three months I would stay. But at that stage, if you recall, there was no work. It was a very depressed time and as it turned out I got a job offer from the *Press* which gave me a bartering position to get a job offer from the *Independent*, so that's where I began.

RG: And you were seven years as deputy editor of the *Evening Herald*. Was that an enjoyable experience?

NH: Absolutely. But because, to a certain extent, I didn't start out with any major career plan, I looked at the fellow in the job above and said, "I wouldn't mind doing that", and it moved on from there .When the opportunities arise I'm a firm believer in taking your chances when you get them; there's no hanging around or prevaricating. You go for it and any time I got an opportunity I went for it. It was a difficult environment to the extent that it changed so dramatically over those seven years. We'd initially begun with deadlines at about 11.20 in the morning for the first edition which went back to about 10.30, then back to 10.00 and now the deadline for the first edition is 9.30, which means a very early start in the mornings, and it's one element I don't miss from the *Herald*. I have to say, getting up at about 4.20 in the morning is difficult!

RG: You say the pressures built up as the *Evening Herald* changed. Has it changed for the better in your view over the past seven or eight years?

NH: I think it has. I think it's a testament to the quality of the people in the *Evening Herald* that we've managed to maintain circulation in an environment where every other newspaper in the western world has lost circulation pretty much. I think there are only three evening papers left in the entire United States. The demand is enormous. You're up against every other media outlet, not alone the morning papers. There's a notion that because the *Evening Herald* is the only evening newspaper in Ireland that it's on its own with an even playing field. I would disagree entirely with that notion because the Herald is up against every morning newspaper on the stands and you're up against every other media outlet, every radio show and against Sky News.

RG: You say the first edition, the national edition, goes to press at 9.30. Therefore it's on the streets at 10.30 or 11.00, or certainly in

Dublin by 11.00, where it's competing with the morning market, the same as the *Evening Standard* in London.

NH: Yes, but you don't have the advantages of the morning market that has all the news from the night before. We can't just turn out the news from the night before and give it a day late and it's stale. So to a certain extent there's a parallel with a Sunday market in that you've got to set the agenda yourself and you've got to find a point of diversity, offering something extra to the readers. Going back to what you said about the *Herald*, I think the *Herald* has achieved that. The demand is that it provides TV listings, it provides sport, it provides news but it also provides all the entertainment that's available as well and I think it's a very thin line constantly making that judgement.

RG: Finding a strong lead at that hour of the morning must be difficult. Obviously what you want to avoid is repeating what the nationals have.

NH: Absolutely! Well the operation begins at 5.30 in the morning so at that point you're looking for information that brings you on. You're listening to *Morning Ireland* or you're following a story in your own way to try and break a new angle on it or equally you're holding onto your own story which you've worked on the previous day and you're presenting that for the first time. So to a certain extent, yes, you don't have any of the advantages of the morning papers but you do have the advantage of being able to do something a bit different.

RG: One case — and you would have been with the *Evening Herald* at the time — was of course the Annabel's Murphy case for the latter half of last year. Many would say that the *Herald* gave excessive coverage to that case. What was the editorial reasoning behind that?

NH: Well, I think it's the same editorial reasoning that would mark a lot of my decisions and that is provocative journalism at the cutting edge of what's happening. But equally you want to be safe. You don't want to stray into the legal minefield that's there and get yourself into difficulty with the courts or be unfair in any way. So we took a conscious decision, a similar decision in relation to the murder investigation in north Dublin late last year. We said we wanted to break the stories on this agenda, we wanted to be in front of everybody else but equally we wanted to be certain that we would be safe. And I think in both cases we achieved that and certainly our readership seems to bear that out because our circulation went up through both periods.

RG: And through the Murphy trial presumably it did as well, whatever about the appeal last week.

NH: In the Annabel's case, I have utmost sympathy for the Murphy family and the tragedy that they suffered, but the Annabel's case has been a phenomenon of our time and the interest in it overall has been enormous and continues to be.

RG: The *Herald* got to the lucky position — or unlucky, I don't know how you would look at it — where analysts in newspapers were reviewing or analysing the *Evening Herald*'s coverage of that case and a lot of people were saying that if this had happened to a working class kid from Darndale or wherever, it wouldn't have received that kind of attention. Is that a legitimate observation in your view?

NH: It may well be but you could make the same argument about Setanta running schools' rugby on television because it's a power base in society and because people who send their children to private schools on the south side of Dublin are generally power brokers of some kind in our society. So there is a legitimacy there in covering the case.

RG: And therefore they're of more interest to the reader than the mythical kid from Darndale?

NH: Well the kid from Darndale may be of interest but there hasn't been a case like this. There hasn't been a case like this where a boy was beaten to death in front of a well-known and well-respected disco outside a well-known hotel in Dublin. That has never happened before. There have been similar cases and they've all received attention of some kind. I think the problem the *Evening Herald* had was how to make this story accessible and to create a compulsion that people felt they needed to read about it and they needed to get the best information they could get and we were providing that and I think that was proved.

RG: Yes, but as we know, part of the appeal was based on prejudicial reporting by newspapers, and I'm not saying the *Herald* was one of those, but just the attention that the case got could have prejudiced the jury. That was part of the defence.

NH: I think Justice Michael White was very careful in that regard and a number of judges would take the view that juries are intelligent enough not to be influenced by what appears in newspapers.

RG: It's difficult though, isn't it?

NH: The alternative is you don't cover the case and we operate in a democracy and we're into another whole debate then.

RG: Obviously we're all swayed by newspapers, whether we like to pretend that we are or we're not, even if it's only gratifying our own political ideologies. People will buy, say, the *Daily Telegraph* for their personal political comforts under the usage and gratifications theory. So, in much the same way, the *Herald*'s coverage, or the coverage of that case all in all, would have definitely had some effect on most people.

NH: Well, I suppose you have to decide: do you want to be commercially minded or do you want to be morally minded? In evidence in the UK, newspaper proprietors are coming from the perspective that it's the power they want to wield and influence and I think they are much more dangerous in a society than newspaper proprietors who want to make money out of their publications.

RG: Indeed. Moving on to your present job as editor of the *Tribune*. What do you see as the main challenges facing you in the *Tribune* at the moment?

NH: I think it's a point you made yourself earlier, Roger. You're faced with a forest of newspapers on a Sunday and the difficulty is that sometimes it becomes a chore to read them. So therefore what we want to do in the *Sunday Tribune* — and I think that I'm very fortunate in that I've come into a very talented team of journalists who are very loyal to the publication and very positive about the future — is to make our paper eminently more readable, to have a factor that compels people to want to read it, to provide enough diversity that keeps them intellectually challenged, that keeps them informed and to provide columnists and opinion that is different and that is a point of differentiation to other titles.

RG: So are you staying with much the same sort of editorial policy, given the market that the *Tribune* is clearly aimed at, the ABC1s?

NH: As I mentioned earlier, we have very loyal readers. Up to 70 per cent of our readers are the ABC1s, as the marketing people call them, so an editor that would come in and mess with that, in my view, would be an absolute lunatic. What I'm there to do is to increase circulation, hopefully by providing more diversity and better stories.

RG: When you say diversity, do you mean diversity of story or diversity of presentation?

NH: I think both to be honest, Roger. I think you've got to have optimum readability in terms of your design and the format of the paper. I think readers are subconsciously very sophisticated in their view of that. But I think diversity in terms of reflecting people's lives. I mean the old models of "father goes to work, mother stays at home" are pretty much obsolete in our society. So there's a whole lot of other things going on out there that need to be reflected in terms of issues people have, dilemmas they have about parenting, relationships, lifestyle issues, as well as politics and the news agenda. I mean the North is turning into a very interesting story again and for a long time, I think, in the south, people's eyes glazed over when you mentioned the North. But that whole political spectrum is fascinating again.

RG: Well it's something one of your very good writers, Diarmuid Doyle, has covered immaculately, I would say, over the years; particularly his analysis of Sinn Féin/IRA.

NH: I think people trust the *Tribune* and I think that's a very important thing that we would not provide any reason for them to doubt us in any way in our coverage.

RG: And there is reader loyalty?

NH: Absolutely; there's very strong reader loyalty which is very reassuring for me as editor.

RG: But the figures have dropped a bit, haven't they?

NH: The figures have dropped slightly but the figures have dropped overall in newspapers in Ireland and the competition is intense. I mean there's 15 or 16 newspapers out there on a Sunday to choose from. Our job is to ensure that our readers are satisfied with the package they're getting. Hopefully we will entice some new readers because everybody wants to develop a bit of strength, get some more resources and get a bit of wind at your back and be able to spend some more money on the news agenda.

RG: And it's become even more competitive, I would have thought, since the English newspapers have introduced Irish editions — *The Sunday Times* being, perhaps, the best example of that. They have their own office so they're turning out an Irish newspaper, whatever about the magazine. That must have added pressure too?

NH: Well they're turning out Irish pages in some instances. I wouldn't go so far as to say they're turning out an Irish newspaper. And yes of course it increases the pressure, but I think what we're offering is an Irish perspective on the Irish situation. We're a newspaper based entirely here. Our circulation is split somewhat 50–50 between Dublin and the country so we're offering a nationwide perspective.

RG: We read about unrest in the *Tribune* among the workers. Is that all gone away?

NH: Well, I haven't come across unrest so far, but I'm only three weeks into the job, Roger, so I haven't upset too many people yet.

RG: No, I think it would be a tough task if you had to go in and start sorting out union problems before anything else, but presumably that is not part of your brief at the moment?

NH: Well, there's a whole infrastructure there to deal with industrial relations matters. I see my job as the news agenda, first and foremost, and it is good news stories that will drive good newspapers and then every other element has got to be of the same standard.

RG: Now one of the obvious things — and I mentioned it earlier — is that you are one of two women editors of a national newspaper. Did you find it a hard task to get to the top, harder than a male, and do you believe in the "glass ceiling"?

NH: I think that to get to be an editor of a newspaper you've got to be very driven, full-stop, whether you're male or female. You've got to put in the effort and the commitment has got to be there. You've got to want it very badly. That's ultimately what it's about. It's about wanting it more than the next person and certainly if that's the case, yes, I have wanted it more, I feel, than a lot of my peers and a lot of them are male. I don't believe it is an even playing field. I do think that the demands are different for women. I think that there are other considerations. I have three children and, in a sense, I think that has made me more driven because I've got a family situation that's very stable and my work–life balance is important to me. So therefore the time that I'm at work I put everything into it. But equally I think you've got to have a life beyond that as well. What's interesting is it's a sort of a non-issue that there's a second woman who's an editor of a national newspaper, and we're catching up with the UK and with America.

$\mathcal{F}$ergal $\mathcal{K}$eane

$\mathcal{F}$ ergal Keane is one of the best-known news broadcasters in both Ireland and Britain,, reporting for the BBC for many years from the world's most troubled areas, such as Rwanda during its horrific period of war and genocide; South Africa in the days of apartheid, and Kosovo. His reporting style is both unique and controversial, tinged, as it often is, with emotion. For this he has come under criticism by the journalistically traditional. Take it as you will, but it clearly works, so much so that he was named overall winner of the Amnesty International Press Awards in 1993 and the Amnesty Television Award the following year for his investigation of Rwandan genocide. However, the dangers of reporting from war zones has had a personal effect on him and I wondered if this was the root cause of his self-confessed alcoholism.

RG: As I said in my intro, your reporting style has come in for criticism by some. Does this worry you at all?

FK: No, not at all. There's an awful lot of "thou shalt" around the place. You should do this or you should be like that. I'm not in the business of conforming to other people's expectations. I'm in the business of telling things as I see them and if that's in Rwanda, describing things as evil — a highly emotive term, some might say — or describing apartheid which I experienced in South Africa before black majority rule, if I describe that as evil then, so be it. My job is not to be there to play up to some expectation of a report that appeals to a small number of English critics in right-wing magazines like *The Spectator* which believes that you should go in for a journalism that's "on the one hand this and on the other hand that". I don't believe in that. I believe that you have to call it as it is from your own knowledge.

RG: In traditional journalism, or certainly in journalism schools, you're always taught to be objective and not to offer your own opinion when reporting. But you've eschewed that.

FK: Yes; but what I do believe is that you have to be fair. Fairness is the key. So, for example, if I'm sent to South Africa, as I was in 1990 to report on the death of apartheid, it's absolutely fair to report apartheid as something evil. But it would be wrong for me to become a cheerleader for the ANC or equally to ignore the fears of the majority of the white population. If people look at my journalism they will always see a concern for people who don't have a voice or are stigmatised or demonised. If you look at what I did in South Africa, for example, I spent an awful lot of my time talking to the Afrikaner farmers who generally, in the media, were given very short shrift. I tried to be fair to them and I'm very, very wary of a kind of journalism which states that you can only do it one way. It's incredible apart from anything else.

RG: Your latest book is a personal memoir, *All of These People.* You were quoted in *The Guardian* as jocosely saying this was your midlife re-think and that 44 is an age at which, and I quote you, "you buy a Porsche and take up with a Jennifer, or you write a memoir". Why did you choose the latter?

FK: I couldn't afford the Porsche and my wife would have killed me if I'd gone off with a Jennifer! But seriously, I think it is an age where someone like me, who's spent a great deal of his time in conflict zones and who on occasion has faced the possibility of death — a violent death — must stop and take stock. In my case it came nearly six years after I decided to give up drinking as an element of my war zone life. And so I stopped and I was taking a long hard look at myself. It actually started out as a book about the state of the world.

RG: A modest undertaking . . .

FK: Yes, exactly, and when I read some of it I was questioning the grandiosity of me standing on the top of a mountain lecturing people about the state of the world and it became instead a journey inwards and it went to three drafts — three drafts of me wondering how much of what had happened to me I could tell. Eventually I ended up with a book that I think is fairly soul-searching and tells some unpalatable truths of the kind of world that I operated in and lived in.

RG: You mentioned your drinking and you've obviously been very open about it. You retired from drinking in 1999, I think, but you're also the son of an alcoholic. Do you think that this was a sort of genetic pass-on or something that was caused by the pressures of reporting from war zones?

FK: Listen, you could look at the past and look at the job I took and say, "Oh God, I wouldn't be an alcoholic but for the job I'm in". But I'm not up for that; that's nonsense. I'm an alcoholic because I'm an alcoholic, you know? It's in me and where it came from in my life doesn't really interest me. It's my responsibility. I used the phrase there a moment ago, "I'm an alcoholic" — just as my father was. But we're both many other things as well. I picked up a tabloid this morning and it was discussing the book. It said I won't die of drink like my Dad, or words to that effect. But that's a cartoon image of who I am. One of the things which the book tries to do is . . . well, obviously it assesses my alcoholism in a fairly honest way but what it also does is look at the kind of other motivations for a foreign correspondent — a person who went to dangerous places to tell difficult stories, and key to that was the influence of my father and mother. They were both very idealistic people, people who believed in talking to me and they did that very passionately. And I hope people can see beyond the cartoon image of the alcoholic to someone who was, in my father's case certainly, a very complex person but also one of the bravest people I've known.

RG: I want to focus on your father for a moment. It seemed to me that he had a successful career as an actor whilst being an alcoholic and you say that the family split because of that alcoholism when you were 11, so you were obviously from a divided home. How much access did you have to your father or did you stay with your mother all the time?

FK: We stayed at home while my father continued to live in Dublin, but I did see him regularly. He wrote. He was fantastic about that. One of the things I remember about him is his beautiful writing and I still have some of his letters. He was always a presence. I think in my later years, when I was by myself, and this was in the 1980s, I drifted away from him because I was, at that stage, angry about the past and I was too alienated from him and of course I was heading down the road to alcoholism myself. So he was a kind of warning, but it was a conversation I didn't want to have and when he died, when he died I . . . realised over a period of time that I missed him and that I loved him more than I'd ever, ever expected.

RG: He died in 1990, isn't that right? You say that both he and your mother taught you to champion the underdog. Do you believe that that is one of the reasons why you were attracted to reporting from war zones?

FK: I think so. I mean psychologists will tell you that the reasons you go to these places is that you're trying to prove to yourself that you can survive over and over again. But I think there's a deeper thing. There was that passion to find people who are shut out, who don't make the headlines, who are voiceless. It came directly from them — my mother and father — and it has been the driving motivation of my life as a journalist. It comes back to the issue of emotion and objectivity. You know, most of the emotion that I've put on the screen is other people's. Telling their stories, not my own.

RG: Yes, but it's clear the way it affects you.

FK: It does affect you — the journalism I do. For example, if you witnessed the Rwanda genocide, the way that affects you is like something that goes onto the screen, something you take away with you. It comes back in your dreams. You think about it in hotel rooms at four in the morning. You expect it.

RG: And can you ever expunge it from your mind?

FK: Look, you get on with living and I have a wonderful, wonderful life, a great family life. But of course it never goes away and in a sense it never should. How could something like the murder of nearly a million people and witnessing some of the mounds of corpses, the people being rounded up . . . No, no, I would be inhuman if that went away.

RG: In the eighties you reported from South Africa. What sort of specific changes have you seen in the country from the time that apartheid was removed?

FK: It's incredible. There's obviously the physical changes in the first place. When I first went there it was in 1984 — I was working for RTÉ at the time — you saw signs that said "whites only". You saw beaches and I could see black people standing looking at the beach and not being allowed to go on to them. It was an incredibly cruel system where you had a secret police that destroyed the lives of millions of people, that killed people in their thousands. You go back there now and the critical thing is the spirit emerging in black people. Young black people who don't feel they're second best. Who haven't been made to feel they're second best and who are determined to build their own country. It's absolutely wonderful.

RG: I've only been there once but the impression I got, and this was only about three years ago, is that they're very willing to forgive.

FK: Yes. It's astonishing. When you look at this country and, you know, you grew up as I did, both of us grew up in the post-Civil War generation and can remember that kind of bitterness that travelled and lingered down through families and political parties and found its way into the Dáil, with people shouting "blueshirt" or whatever still. But then you go to South Africa and you realise that only a decade ago you saw it in action — apartheid — and now it's in the past. It is absolutely phenomenal what people have been able to achieve there in a short time.

RG: In the book you say you were terrified in Iraq. Being in the thick of any war is undoubtedly very scary. But having covered so many so called hot wars, is there not a stage where the war-weary journalist becomes, if not inured to it, at least used to it?

FK: Yes. And I could feel that happening to me. You fly around the world from one hell-hole to another and apart from anything else you get an incredibly screwed-up idea of what the world is really like. You know what I mean? You can forget there is a whole raft of people in countries around the world who are living normal, decent lives; who are building things instead of destroying them and that's one of the things that worries me about the whole business of being slotted as a war correspondent. Because that is only part of what human beings do. It's a professional danger because you come back with questions about humanity, a view of humanity, that is very dark. If you don't wake up and see that there are roses to be smelt too . . . and I've had to do that to myself on several occasions. And I've now come to the conclusion I can't go to wars any more. You know, those hot wars, I just can't do that any more.

RG: You've put a sort of steadfast "no" on that, have you?

FK: An absolutely vehement "no"! And I need to say it publicly on programmes like this because people like you will be there to hammer me if I even dream of going and doing it again.

RG: So you're going to stick by it. Why?

FK: Because of a couple of things. I don't want to die. That's a fundamental reason and I've had two very good friends of mine this past year, one of them only three weeks ago, Kate Peyton, murdered in Somalia. She was shot in the back. You know, only three weeks before that, I was sitting at her dinner table in Johannesburg talking about the house she was building with her fiancé and of the little child she was adopting. I don't want my children standing next to my coffin. Nobody will ever be able to answer to them or tell them that it was worth it. Because he did this or because he brought that truth out and it was worth it. Absolutely not!

RG: But where does that leave you? As you say, you don't want to be ghettoised as a war zone reporter.

FK: Well I think I allowed that happen to me.

RG: So how have you now shifted your emphasis in your work?

FK: One of the things that I really want to do is related to what I mentioned to you a while ago — that you can get a very skewed view of the world. I want to kind of counteract that and I want to go to Africa and tell stories — not good news, I hate the idea of going and telling good news, but just news. And the thing is for too long we have ignored the "other news". The fact that, for example, in a country like Mozambique they're building a successful, functioning democracy out of decades of brutal warfare. Go to South Africa and look at what people are achieving there. There are many stories to be told, many really good stories.

RG: Indeed. Now, just to switch emphasis for the moment, as an Irishman abroad and also as a well-respected journalist, your opinion on Northern Ireland must be sought continuously, is it?

FK: It is! Is that a dangerous thing?

RG: And how do you respond?

FK: Well, you'll be aware of certain difficulties the BBC has had in the last year or so about journalists offering their own opinions . . .

RG: . . . Well yes indeed . . .

FK: . . . where they were wrong! So one treads carefully. But I think what I can offer is a kind of armed analysis, if you like, and say that I think we're living through the most extraordinary few weeks. Not just about Northern Ireland, but as a history of the island as a whole. When we spoke about the Civil War and the kind of country you and I grew up in, that country, was defined by fear. Fear of establishments, whether they're political or religious; fear of being seen to step out of line. And I think that country of fear, north and south, is going. And when you see people taking on an organisation like the IRA in the way that they've done — the McCartney sisters have done — that's phenomenal. Ryszard Kapuscinski, one of the foreign correspondents I admire most, had a book about the Shah of Iran called *Shah of Shahs* and he said that the moment comes when people lose their fear, and nothing is ever the same.

RG: And you think that that's what's happening? Because quite clearly one of the major fears is intimidation and that has turned 22 people blind to a quite horrendous event. So how do you justify your rationalisation that fear is now on the wane?

FK: Because of those remarkable sisters; and I think that they set an example for people to follow. Nothing about this process, from its beginning, has been easy. You and I will remember when John Hume first went to talk to Adams and the kind of controversy that erupted around that. You know we have moved a long way from then. And I think the McCartney sisters will be seen, in years to come, as among the most remarkable Irish patriots. They really will, because it starts with people like that. It will take time but other people will lose their fear because of that example. I passionately believe it.

RG: Yes, certainly what they're doing is incredibly brave and not before its time, a lot of people would say as well. But generally, how do you feel Ireland is reported abroad? You were saying that there is always the trouble that gets reported, you know, worldwide be it Rwanda, be it South Africa; that we hear about the wars, we hear about the horrors but we don't necessarily hear the good news. How, as somebody who is abroad a lot, do you feel Ireland is reported internationally?

FK: Well I think that's interesting. You started off with a stereotype of the troubles and the fighting Irish or the Irish who were fleeing their country in emigration and now we have the Ireland as a success story template. So the media tends to like to adapt to a template. And it's not just Ireland, it's everywhere I see it; you fit a particular template onto a country. But you miss a lot of the sophisticated undercurrents in a country in doing that. I would have to say that reading the British press, if you compare it to the kind of treatment that we got as a country in the seventies, particularly when the Troubles were at their height — much of it racist, there is absolutely no doubt about it. But there has been a huge change. And that has been about a revolution in the attitudes in England and the peace process but a huge part of it is about our national self-assertiveness. We're not snivelling anymore. We're not ashamed of ourselves. We don't go around feeling there's snots on our coat, you know.

RG: The inferiority complex has gone . . .

FK: . . . has gone, and that's a marvellous thing. You know it's great to go around London, to go to events and find so many Irish people in key positions, doing well there and projecting a vision of us that is confident, that is outward-looking.

RG: No longer the Paddies on the building sites, so to speak. Now, the title of your book *All of These People* comes from a Michael Longley poem, is that right? Why this title?

FK: Michael Longley is to me such a fantastic poet — Michael from Belfast. And he wrote a poem . . . when I was living in Belfast there was a murder on the Lisburn Road in an ice-cream shop. The man who ran the ice-cream shop was murdered. It shocked all of us who live around that community and Michael, in his poem *All of These People* talks about the effect of violence on a community, but also the power of a community to fight back — much like I was talking about with the McCartney sisters. The opening of the poem says, "I don't know who it was who said the opposite of war is not so much peace as civilisation." And I've looked at my past and my family. I've looked at the places I've gone to and reported on and the defining thing about them is the need to be civilised. And my parents were civilised people. The people I met in South Africa, in Rwanda, who shone for me were civilised people and the book is about all of those people.

RG: I want to take you back to *Letter to Daniel*, which stirred up an incredible wave of emotion, not just in these islands, but worldwide. What motivated you to write that?

FK: Funny, it didn't come from me. A phone call came from London, from the editor of a programme called *From Our Own Correspondent*, and he asked me would I write a piece about what it's like to have a child in a foreign country — somewhere like Hong Kong in the last years of the Empire. I was initially reluctant for those very reasons that you spoke about at the start, you know, getting too personal, and then I just sat down and he rang me again and I said OK, I'll do it. And I wrote it in one sitting. It just came out as it was — and that's where it came from.

RG: And you say that you didn't have to re-draft that for the most part . . .

FK: . . . it just told itself.

RG: And it has certainly been a very lasting thing. In fact, I can remember the time it first went out on *From Our Own Correspondent*. I remember listening to it and how it arrested me. So what are you involved in now, what are you actually doing in the BBC?

I know you say you're going to go to Mozambique and various other places but . . .

FK: It's interesting, you can report on human rights without having to be in the zone of bullets and bombs. So I'm doing an investigation into the UN Security Council and Darfur. A lot of that will take place in New York, for example, and deconstructing why we've allowed these people to be abandoned and that'll be an hour-long film for the BBC and that's very rewarding. You just keep digging away and it's a very forensic style of journalism you know — just getting documents, trying to get a whistleblower to speak, all of that. And that's exciting; it's great to be able to do that.

RG: Finally, any thoughts on coming home?

FK: I never left.

Gene Kerrigan

*J*ournalists come and journalists go, but Gene Kerrigan has been at the forefront of his trade for nigh on 30 years. The opinionated columnist started off with Magill and his views have become provocative reading every week on the back page of the Sunday Independent. He has been unflinching in his common sense approach to questioning, pillorying and, when warranted, ridiculing our politicians of whichever ideology. He has done his fair share of investigative journalism, but is more comfortable, perhaps, commentating and analysing events and revelations in the world of politics and public life. At the time Gene was my guest on "Under the Spotlight" his first novel, Little Criminals, had just been published by Vintage. I was curious to know how he had enjoyed his first attempt at writing fiction.

RG: This is your first novel. Why the change to fiction writing after years of dealing with fact?

GK: It's not a change, it's an addition. The old joke is that half of the journalists in Ireland have half a novel in their desk drawer and I used to have one twenty years ago, but it was terrible. So I decided to wait until I knew I could do it well and I did it as well as I could before I showed it to anyone. I showed it to an agent in London and he thought it was very good so here we are.

RG: Can you give us a flavour of the book?

GK: Well it's a crime novel set in Dublin. It's slightly unusual in that it uses the same techniques, the same approach, as any crime novel set in New York or California or London or wherever. It doesn't have an American investigator coming in and it's set here in, I think, a recognisable Ireland. It's about a major crime carried out by small-time criminals and the effects it has on them. I wanted to portray them as people who have families and mortgages and ambitions but who are quite ruthless in what they do. Then there are the people they affect, the police and the bystanders, who are affected by it as well. I wanted to get a cross-section of Ireland.

RG: So it delves into their home lives and those affected by their crimes?

GK: It's more about the people and it could have been any crime, but as it happens it's a kidnap.

RG: A crime we're familiar with in this country over the last 30 years. Your publishers say it is set in an Ireland where the agenda is no longer dictated by Catholic bishops or paramilitaries. Some would say that the latter wouldn't be true because of recent events. I'm referring to the kidnapping of families of bank officials in order to carry off large-scale robberies.

GK: But it isn't that they are setting the agenda anymore. These events, I think, look very much like the remnants and leftovers of something that happened up to the mid-nineties and what's been happening since then is trying to find a way of winding it up and you're getting all kinds of things spinning off from it. There's a kind of tug of war between certain factions. But they're not setting the agenda any more. They did set the agenda in the eighties, certainly. A lot of government policy had to do with pushing it aside and keeping it on the other side of the border and therefore a lot of policies down here were influenced by that, I think.

RG: But the kidnapping in Cork this week — I don't want to get sidetracked too much by this — but you reckon that this was a renegade, breakaway faction?

GK: Well, as I say, there's no shortage of kidnappings, whether it's in an armoured car that they're held in for a short time or whatever. This seems to be a technique in fashion at the moment. It's not a particularly political thing. A lot of it has to do with the growth of a crime industry over the last 15 or 20 years.

RG: So the protests of innocence from Sinn Féin leaders, from your point of view, would be genuine?

GK: No, I don't see it that way. I think they played a double game for the last ten years and it's coming back to bite them, in that they'd nothing to do with this thing, yet they had something to do with it in that they could influence it. But now it's going in a particular direction which they don't seem to be able to influence and they're in a spin.

RG: Which means that they can't deliver at the end of the day?

GK: It may mean that I don't know, in fact I don't think anybody knows. There's a lot of very categorical statements being

made about what's happening. An awful lot of categorical statements have been made over the last 20 years, which turned out to
be nonsense. It's very easy to categorise this as one thing or another. I think it's something which was part of what we were for
30 years and is now in the process of disintegration. But I don't
think it's all over yet.

RG: Well it certainly doesn't seem to have true signs of being all
over, no matter how you look at it. For 30 years you have been
dealing with criminal matters and, indeed, quasi-criminal matters,
if you add in the political dimension. How close have you got over
the years to those involved, to the protagonists of major stories?

GK: Not very. One of the things I tend to do is cover stories
which have broken. I'm not the kind of journalist who breaks stories, therefore I'm not knocking on people's doors in the middle of
the night asking them to give me an off-the-record comment on
something. It's a different kind of journalism. I've covered a
whole lot of stories from the Kerry babies onwards, those sort of
things. At one stage I'd a reputation of being some kind of investigative journalist. I'm not.

RG: That probably sprang from your *Magill* days, going back
20 years?

GK: It did. There were a whole lot people there, Vincent
Browne obviously and the late Derek Dunne, now they were investigative in their approach. I did some investigative work, but
nothing remarkable. My talents were in a different direction in
terms of writing about the things in a comprehensible way and
going into depth.

RG: In that depth, particularly when it comes to terrorist organisations or their allies, do they tend to come to you when it is to their
advantage, in other words when they are seeking a PR opportunity?

GK: No, not to me in particular. I've had the experience, which I think a lot of journalists have had, of talking to a Sinn Féin leader and then there's a slight pause, a break, and then I'm talking to an IRA leader, which I think a lot of journalists have had down through the years. However, I think there are quite a number of journalists who were far better at covering the North. If these organisations want to put out a story, there are any number of journalists in Belfast. I've never had the pleasure of somebody knocking on my door saying, "Do you want to have an exclusive on where we're going to bomb next?", or whatever.

RG: Well not everyone would welcome such a knock on the door!

GK: Well I know I'm glad I haven't!

RG: Over the years, both directly in your analysis pieces on the back pages of the *Sunday Independent* and in a satirical or sarcastic style, you've managed to communicate the feelings of a large section of this society. Are they your own true beliefs with regard to, say, paramilitary action and certain political parties?

GK: Well I haven't written all that much about paramilitary action over the years and particularly over the last ten years or so. An awful lot of people are writing about it. A lot of them aren't terribly good at it and I decided that there are enough people on that pitch so I've chosen to write about other things. It's not an area that I've specialised in.

RG: But you have written on the hypocrisy of the Sinn Féin/ IRA allegiance, or lack thereof, as they will tell you.

GK: Yes, for instance it's 20 years ago now that the late Derek Dunne and I wrote a book on the Nicky Kelly case. We went into it in some detail and it had to do with the effects of those things on how we live and the effect on the people who went to jail for a crime that they didn't commit, rather than an overall analysis of where the North is going, on which I haven't written because I've absolutely no expertise. I would tend to write on the effects of those kind of events rather than predictions of where the North goes next.

RG: But that is largely what the reader in the South wants, particularly the more generalised, non-specific political interest type reader.

GK: As I say there's absolutely no shortage of people who do that and some of them are very good and some of them are not and it's not an area that I've specialised in.

RG: What is your overall view of the *Sunday Independent*, because it has made its reputation, or re-invented itself, on strong criticism of Sinn Féin/IRA. Having been, back in the seventies, a very strong investigative paper — take the Irish Hospital Sweeps exposé, for example. So what are your views of the paper now? Obviously that is a difficult question as they are your employers, I grant you.

GK: One of the things in journalism and about journalism I've noticed over the years is that it's very, very easy to acquire a reputation for something. For instance I acquired, as I said earlier, a reputation as an investigative journalist which I'm not. I'm very good at other things but I'm not good at that. People will say look at the *Sunday Independent* in the seventies and say it did this or that. It's not so long ago, for instance, that Liam Collins did the exposé on AIB which has reaped hundreds of millions of euro for the Exchequer and I give Liam a pat on the back every time I see him because he probably brought down our taxes by a couple of pence. But what I think has happened in journalism now is that it's expanded. It has taken in quite a lot of different sections. For instance you get analysis now that you didn't get 20 or 30 years ago, or that you only got in a magazine. Newspapers have expanded into magazine areas and at the same time you're getting the kind of exposés that have been done on the scandals. Let's remember that an awful lot of what has come out in the last ten years or so has been media-driven and quite a lot of it has been *Sunday Independent*-driven.

RG: You used to work in a cinema before you ever went into journalism. Was cinema your first interest?

GK: Oh no. It was my first wage packet. I was about fourteen and I needed work back in the sixties, as so many of us did. It was just after the previous wave of emigration. An awful lot of my friends and my older brothers had to leave the country to get work. Things improved marginally then and I worked in the cinema for twelve years, I showed movies and I loved movies. When that was over I more or less drifted for a while and I ended up in journalism.

RG: You joined *Magill*?

GK: I'd written freelance pieces. I wrote a piece for *The Irish Times* and I wrote a number of pieces for *Hot Press*. Then I wrote freelance for *Magill* before I joined the staff.

RG: And in fact you were writing on cinema in the early days for *Magill*, weren't you?

GK: I wrote a couple of things, reviews, but nothing very much.

RG: But what spurred you on to journalism, having, as you say, earned your first few bob in a cinema. What brought about that transition into journalism?

GK: I loved journalism as a reader and it never occurred to me that I could get into it because there were, well, you know, particular routes into journalism and I hadn't a clue as to how I would get into it. In the late seventies there was an expansion of the economy. There were a number of things which came in coincidentally and a number of magazines were going around at that time — *Hot Press, In Dublin, Magill* — which are still going. *Hibernia* was still coming out and it was a time when, if you wanted to advertise a car in colour, for instance, you couldn't do it in the newspapers because they didn't have colour technology, so the magazine was there and *Magill* triumphed on that kind of thing. I didn't know it at the time, Vincent Browne never told me, but looking back on it, the magazine lived from month to month and one investor would drop out and another one would come in. It had an appearance on the outside of being a very solid magazine and journalistically it was very solid but we lived hand to mouth, I suppose, looking back on it. But it didn't seem that way at the time and it was very, very enjoyable

RG: You said an interesting thing there in relation to your love of journalism. You said you loved journalism as a reader. Very often people will remark that journalists, by and large, tend to write stories for other journalists, rather than keeping the reader in mind. Is that fair criticism or not?

GK: I think we all fall into that one from time to time. My only answer is that when you write a sentence, you tend to hope that the reader will continue to the end of that sentence and if you do it well enough, they will. If you then work on the next sentence, they may stick with that as well. Hopefully you come across a sufficient number of very interesting stories that will grip the reader. It's the story. You can write as brilliantly as you like, but if you don't get the stories, you don't have the reader.

RG: Sure, from that point of view it's absolutely right. Now one of the people that you mentioned is Vincent Browne whom you worked with in *Magill* and he was also instrumental in setting up the *Sunday Tribune* and you went with him. A lot of people have stories varying between humour through to pathos and antagonism, in regard to Vincent Browne. You've obviously found working with him to be a positive experience as you stuck with him through both *Magill* and the *Sunday Tribune*.

GK: I think Vincent has been a major player in the media. He's done great things in the media over the last 25 years or so. All the stories about him being difficult to work with are true. I found him difficult to work with from time to time. But you don't tend to remember that kind of thing. We all have arguments with our bosses and I sometimes look back at passionate arguments that I had with him and wonder what they were about. At the time they were heartfelt and it was a pressure cooker in a way, in *Magill* and the *Tribune*. Remember, they were very independent publications and eventually *Magill* was earning quite good money. It was solid enough and it's still around today in a different form. The *Sunday Tribune* is still around, again, in a different form. It was a difficult period, I imagine, commercially, and yet they were trying to do interesting things journalistically so that kind of pressure shows and maybe you're better off with that kind of pressure rather than being comfortable and smug.

RG: What are your views of Vincent Browne's latest publication, *Village*? Very independent is how you described both *Magill* and the *Sunday Tribune* at the time he was there, but how do you view *Village*?

GK: I thought it was wobbly for the first three or four issues. I thought it had too many things in it. But I think it has settled down and I think it has focused itself better and I buy it every week. As you flick through a magazine, and this is the criterion by which I would judge a magazine, you spot something and you say, "Oh yeah, I'll mark that and come back to it", and you do. You end up, as you flick through a magazine, with three or four pieces that you know you'll go back to and read them in depth. He's managed to do that. Again, I haven't seen Vincent for years so I don't know, but I imagine that it's breaking new ground commercially as well as journalistically and it's something that I very much hope succeeds.

RG: Yes, it's good to have a magazine like that on the market. Having asked you about *Village*, I have to get a quick opinion on, as you referred to it, the new *Magill* which is still around but in a new format and with a new political slant under its new editor Eamonn Delaney. So what are your views on it as you were there at its birth so to speak?

GK: When we were there in the earlier days in the eighties, we worked to a large extent to a dissenting and questioning voice and I think that's needed today. I think Ireland is quite smug and it's what we've got in the current *Magill*, and fair play to them, and good luck to them. I still buy it out of journalistic loyalty — but it seems to be a very smug voice. It seems to think that the world is run by lefties, liberals and feminists and what it needs is people who will attack that. I think that there's enough of that in the mainstream media. It's very much a mainstream media attitude and we have a very healthy media doing that already.

RG: The thing said about its editorial policy, which would tend to be capitalist, right-wing. It's appealing to a younger audience because, post-Thatcher, you'll find the average student is no longer the left-wing anarchist that the student was, say 20, 30 years ago and certainly an acquisitive dimension has come into that age group.

GK: That may be true. I imagine that there's still quite a lot of questioning that goes on among young people and I don't think you can divide it into young and old, but what I would question is whether it's necessary. I think most people who look back on the eighties would say that a questioning voice was necessary then and I think *Magill* fulfilled that role. I think that one of the things you've got in this country is quite a lot of smug voices and maybe there's a book to be written on being a cheerleader for the smug brigade. One of the things I find is that they're fighting arguments that were won by the right wing ten or 15 years ago. If you look, for instance, at the right wing in Britain or in America, they're having different kinds of arguments about where they go themselves, where they take people. In some ways in America it's quite frightening at the moment, the way they see judges for instance as targets, literally in some cases, and judges are going around with bodyguards. The right wing here doesn't seem to have got into that yet. They seem to be still fighting the old arguments that they were fighting in the eighties. From my point of view it keeps them busy and that's fine.

$\mathcal{D}$amien $\mathcal{K}$iberd

*A*lthough his journalistic background is print, Damien Kiberd made a seamless transition to radio broadcasting and he has presented Lunchtime with Damien Kiberd *for* Newstalk 106 *since the station started in April 2002. His show has become essential listening for intellectual debate on news and current affairs and it has piled on the listeners over the past three years. Damien earned himself a prestigious PPI Award in 2004. He started his journalistic career with the* Irish Press *before moving to the* Sunday Tribune *which he left after two years to establish and edit* The Sunday Business Post. *Some years ago he sold his interest in the paper, having built a healthy circulation. He was then approached by Newstalk 106 to present the lunchtime show. Damien had just been appointed Station Editor of Newstalk 106 at the time of this interview. But having edited* The Sunday Business Post *for many years, why did he want to go back into the fray of editorial de-cision making?*

RG: You're well-known in print and now you've shifted to ra-dio; in fact you shifted to radio three years ago. How are you find-ing the difference?

DK: Well, radio is completely different. It's much more flexible and easier to work with than printing a newspaper. In newspa-pers there are about seven different tasks you have to do right. You have to distribute it right, you have to print it properly, you have to have good editorial ideas, you have to have motivated staff, very tight financial control, you have to generate revenue — all that kind of stuff. But radio is quite simple.

RG: Most managing directors of radio stations would say that you have to do all of that as well.

DK: Well from my point of view I've gone to a situation where I've just really concentrated on running my programme, so I find it's a lot more flexible; radio is a flexible medium, you can turn around a programme with ten different items everyday. It's great I think.

RG: Do you prefer it to your days in newspapers? What you were really describing were the responsibilities of being a proprie-tor as well as the editor of *The Sunday Business Post*.

DK: Yes, that's absolutely true. One of the things I liked best about newspapers goes back a long, long time ago when I was a reporter on a daily newspaper. I liked the whole way of life where you started at maybe ten or eleven in the morning and you worked through to ten or eleven at night. You worked long days but you got a great kick out of it because I worked in a newspaper company that had morning, evening and Sunday newspapers.

RG: This was the Irish Press Group.

DK: The old Irish Press Group, where there was an industrial atmosphere. There were big, huge printing machines in the basement, there was a hot metal composing room, a case room and so forth. It was an absolutely fantastic atmosphere. They were strong, powerful newspapers that you could get stories into and you could measure yourself against the competition. It was a very good place to be and I liked that a lot. I like radio very much as well, because there's also scope for good team effort.

RG: There is, absolutely. Just going back to the *Irish Press*, at the time when you were working there, Tim Pat Coogan would have been the editor, isn't that right?

DK: He was, yes, for all of the time that I was there actually. I worked there for eight years.

RG: Politically you'd have been at one with Tim Pat, would you?

DK: Well, yeah I thought his ideas were very, very good. The paper itself was quite radical. People who didn't read the *Irish Press* always said it was a Fianna Fáil paper. People who did read it knew it wasn't a Fianna Fáil paper and that it was capable of breaking stories on a daily basis that embarrassed Fianna Fáil governments — much more so, I think, than *The Irish Times* or the *Irish Independent* at that time. So Tim Pat ran a very free and independent newspaper and I kind of concurred with him in many ways. I also concurred with a lot of his views and ideas, obviously, about the Anglo-Irish issue.

RG: The one accusation you've alluded to there is the notion that the de Valera family imprint was on the papers, but you're saying that wasn't actually the case in reality.

DK: No, every four years we'd have an election and there'd be a sort of a ritualistic editorial saying what great people Fianna Fáil were, but that was about it and I never recall — and I worked there for eight years — the de Valeras interfering in the editorial content. I only remember one evening Major Vivian de Valera, who was the son of the original Dev, came in one evening and he asked me in a rather embarrassed way if I could manage to get a few paragraphs of a speech he'd given in Dáil Éireann about the Wildlife Bill into the paper that night.

RG: Well that was hardly political persuasion or coercion!

DK: No, he was concerned about a certain species of wildlife and he thought it was important that it be highlighted. He was a very nice and polite man.

RG: And what brought you to the *Press* in the first instance?

DK: Pure accident. After I left college I went to work in a bank, the Industrial Credit Company, and I was lending money to factories and after about two years I found it became quite boring to work in a nine-to-five job and I was looking around for something a bit more exciting. There was an ad in the newspaper for a journalist with the *Irish Press*. I applied for the job, I didn't get it because I had no experience of journalism, but I was actually placed number three in the interview. The first person who got the job, took it and then chickened out. The second person got a job in the BBC and they came to me as I was number three and they said, "Would you like this job?" I had nearly forgotten about it at that stage and I said, "Me, work as a journalist? Yeah, OK, I'll do it."

RG: So you weren't deterred by the fact that you were third down the list.

DK: No. I went down in my beautiful suit and tie on my first day and then I realised that it was a kind of a quasi-industrial atmosphere and that I was improperly dressed, but I managed to get into the swing of things quite quickly.

RG: And out of your suit no doubt as well.

DK: Yes, absolutely, threw the tie in the bin . . .

RG: You said you were eight years in the *Irish Press*. When did you leave?

DK: Well I actually did a stint working in the *Sunday Tribune* for two years as well and that I found, after the excitement of the daily paper, was a bit of a turn-off. It was a different pace of work and that was in the late eighties and the editor at the time was Vincent Browne. But it was probably a good paper, an innovative paper in its time but I wasn't as happy as I had been previously when I was working on daily newspapers.

RG: And what were the reasons for your unhappiness in the *Trib*? Anything to do with the main man there?

DK: No, nothing terrible, I was always on good terms with Vincent Browne and we had some good adventures together of a journalistic nature in those two years, lots of stories, good stories that caused a lot of controversy. I just found the pace of working on that paper was slightly different from what I had been used to previously.

RG: More leisurely, presumably, from the daily grind?

DK: I suppose when you're coming into that, it's like coming down off a high. You know when you're working on a daily paper you can turn around editions of papers very quickly. In the old days the Press newspapers used to have four editions for the

Evening Press and two for the *Irish Press* and umpteen editions for the *Sunday Press* and so forth, so it was kind of a very frenetic atmosphere. After leaving the *Sunday Tribune* I got involved with three other people, all journalists.

RG: Yes, there was Aileen O'Toole who was, at that stage, editor of *Business and Finance*, if I remember rightly, wasn't she?

DK: She was, yes, or had been until very recently before the launch of *The Sunday Business Post*. She was the first woman editor of a major magazine, I think. Frank Fitzgibbon . . .

RG: . . . and of course James Morrissey from the *Independent*.

DK: Yes, James had been deputy editor of the *Herald* for a while and he had also been deputy business editor on the *Irish Independent*. Frank Fitzgibbon was a magazine editor. He had edited *Irish Business* and I think he was a senior person within *Business and Finance* and he had been in other publications as well — a great innovator. It all emanated out of a long conversation one day after a long lunch and we decided to set up a newspaper and, of course, everyone in the country said we were completely and utterly nuts, including Gay Byrne, who said on radio that the whole thing would collapse in six months, these people are nuts, they're losing their marbles.

RG: Was the idea alcohol-fuelled at the end of the lunch or had the seeds of creation been in all your minds at the time?

DK: Yes, I think we were all looking around for something to do and we'd been through this dreadful period of the 1980s when the government wrecked the economy and we were all coming out of that and we thought it was a good idea to start a new business. So we put in train the planning process and had hoped to launch it in September of 1989 but we got delayed. In the end it was launched in November 1989 and it was very hard going I must say.

RG: Well you had all been commentators on business and certainly would have known the Irish business scene but by the nature of the four of you, you wouldn't have actually run a business before.

DK: Well Frank became the original Chief Executive of the *Business Post*.

RG: Was he self-elected?

DK: We had a bit of a discussion and decided that this was the best way to divvy out the responsibilities

RG: You mean you all acquiesced!

DK: We acquiesced — I was the editor, James Morrissey was my deputy and Aileen was the news editor and that was the way the thing was organised. But the fun and games started when it came to the financing of the paper.

RG: Yes, getting the finance together was quite a public thing at the time, but just remind the listeners how it all happened.

DK: Well what we decided to do was to create a vehicle under the Business Expansion Scheme, as that would allow people to invest in the new company and get tax relief on their share investments, which was quite common in those days. In other words, if you put in 25 grand or whatever, you'd get tax relief at 42 per cent or whatever the upper rate of tax was — probably a bit higher in those days. We went to a firm of stockbrokers, Riada, which is now ABN Amro, and they organised the financing of the paper successfully and the whole thing was constructed and put together. Detailed business plans were drawn up for the whole venture and we had a printer on board with us, a guy called John Kerry Keane who was participating as a shareholder. He said he'd prefer if we went to a different firm of stockbrokers so we went to Davy Stockbrokers and they in turn raised the money successfully for the venture. A lot of people believed in us you see, Roger. I know by that look on your face that you disbelieve me!

RG: No, no, not at all, I'm just fascinated about the whole thing and what I want to do is come back to the seeds of the newspaper and the first thing you would have had to do was to persuade first Riada and subsequently Davy's that there was a market there for the paper in the first instance. But back to raising the finance for the venture, which you were arranging under the old BES scheme, or what was formerly the BDS scheme, and Riada pulled out of the deal . . .

DK: No, no, they didn't, Roger, they supported it. It was just that one of our backers, a printer, wanted to go to a different firm of stockbrokers and they, in turn, backed the idea and they arranged the financing of it.

RG: So how easy was it? Because presumably you had to present them with a fairly convincing document of market research to show that there was a market there for yet another Sunday on a small market, given that we had our own selection of papers plus Irish editions of the UK papers? It must have been a very hard task to find that niche and to persuade them that that niche was there.

DK: No it wasn't actually because they were business people as well and they were interested in business. Now the idea, originally, was that we would have a paper that would have a circulation of 17,000, growing to 25,000. The circulation is now, by the way, around 55,000, so it's been a roaring success in quite a small country for a business paper. What we said to them was, essentially, every European country, including countries that were far less economically developed than Ireland, such as Portugal, had business newspapers. There was an appetite for them but we created rather conservative circulation projections and we drew up very detailed business plans with cash flows, costs and revenues and so forth.

RG: All of which would have cost you a fair few bob presumably or did you do that all yourselves?

DK: We did a lot of the work ourselves and we drew up, obviously, the editorial plan for the paper and we identified the target market. The fact that it was "niched" as a product was also useful in the sense that we were going to be selling direct into the market that the advertising agencies wanted to target and there was big backing for us. In the end we went with a French company as an investor.

RG: They came on board late, didn't they?

DK: Quite extraordinary, I had been talking to a guy in France called Jean Louis Schreiber, a big European publisher, and he was very interested in the project. The whole thing about the BES scheme fell apart because we couldn't qualify as a manufacturing company for the ten per cent rate of tax which was part of the BES. I was on the phone to Jean Louis and he said, "Well, you know, I'd like to talk to you about investing in the business", and he came over to Ireland on a sort of speculative trip. He'd never been here before but within 24 hours he wanted to invest and the following Wednesday we signed up in Paris in an office on the seventh floor in the Quai des Citroens on a handshake and he said, "You'll have the money in the morning." So that was it.

RG: Fantastic!

DK: It was a rather crazy few weeks.

RG: But then you had the major task of course, as if that task wasn't big enough, of getting the finance to do it. You then had to turn around and pull together an editorial team. OK, you had, between the four of you, a vast amount of experience but you also needed bodies to go out and about.

DK: Absolutely; we got good journalists, very strong, young journalists who were interested in the idea of a new paper. For example, Matt Cooper of Today FM, the former *Tribune* editor, was one of the young people. Also Susan O'Keeffe, whose work was to lead to the Beef Tribunal and various others joined us. Also we'd lots of young people who wanted to sell advertising and so forth, so we had a core staff of about 25 at the beginning. It was rather frenetic to try and get the whole thing put together in time. We got it launched in November 1989 and as a matter of fact, I would say to you, Roger, one of the central things for the first year or two was not so much getting the editorial product right; it was actually convincing advertising people to abandon their sort of conservative ideas. They were stuck with the existing titles and they had to take a chance and put ads into our product.

RG: Yes, but as you say, it was a niche market and the readership would have been very much ABC1 socio-economic grouping. Therefore that niche, in terms of picking off the ad agencies, would have been a bit easier than the other end of the market, I would have thought.

DK: Yes, well certainly getting access and making the argument was easy but people do get set in their ways and they say, "You know, I'm advertising with the *Sunday Press* or the *Sunday Independent*, which have a big circulation, so why should I go with these guys?" Every media organisation, I think, suffers from that kind of inertia of thinking out there in the market place.

RG: "If it works, don't fix it." We all know that it ended up doing very well and is still there as you say, selling 55,000 copies a week. So why did you decide to sell out?

DK: Well, we felt that we had developed and progressed the product by 1997 to the point where it was selling in the mid-30,000 copies each week and it was making profits. We always felt vulnerable because we were small people competing with big people. The Irish Independent Newspaper Group was pouring money into our main opponent, which was the *Sunday Tribune*, and we felt like we needed some kind of market power. Now the strange thing was we were actually approached by a group called Trinity Mirror who expressed interest in buying the newspaper. They had become owners of the *Belfast Telegraph* and they could see the way our print run was growing every few months. They were impressed by the fact that we were increasing the circulation of the newspaper so strongly and they said, "Would you lads be interested if we took a stake or invested in the business?" In the heel of the hunt they basically bought *The Sunday Business Post* in 1997.

RG: Prior to that, Frank Fitzgibbon and James Morrissey had pulled out, leaving you and Aileen O'Toole.

DK: Frank had gone in or around 1991 and James Morrissey, I think, left in 1992, so they were gone about five or six years at the point when all of that happened. But at that stage Barbara Nugent, who was ex-*Tribune*, had joined as Chief Executive of the *Post* and had become a shareholder, so Aileen, Barbara and myself were all shareholders at this stage. It's a very complex history but a German company had come into the frame and had taken up the balance of the shares at that point. The French had dropped away, not for any reasons to do with the *Business Post*, but to do with their own domestic situation in France. They had decided to exit various investments.

RG: Now it had earned a nickname, as you are only too well aware, during its life, as being the "Provisional Business Post", so it's safe to say that you come from a republican viewpoint. Was that problematic during the time in terms of your editorship or editorial policy?

DK: No, it was not. We never had any interference from share-holders of any kind in the editorial policy, not from the French at the beginning — that was one of the great beauties, that the French people didn't know Irish business people — so they weren't being rung up every week by somebody, or taken out onto the golf course and asked, "Can you clip the wings of those people?" The Trinity Mirror people, who are British to the core, never once interfered.

RG: And you were happy enough in the same room with them were you?

DK: Yes, we were fine. There was no editorial interference. And the other thing, Roger, I would say to you is that despite the phobias about strong national feeling in Ireland, an awful lot of business people are very proud of this country and they're very republican. You scratch a lot of business people and you find they're republican.

RG: As was scratched not so many months ago to reveal some people quite high up within the business world. But without dwelling on that, what I want to get on to now is Newstalk. You had left the world of print at that stage and presumably you were resting on your laurels a bit and you had every right to so do and then you were approached by Newstalk, or did you approach Newstalk?

DK: Well our illustrious friend Daire O'Brien, one of the world's great broadcasters, had said to me prior to Christmas of

2001, "Damo, would you be interested in doing a few radio pro-grammes?" And I said, "Well sure Daire, if it happens." I didn't really take him too seriously at that point. I had just left the *Business Post* and I didn't really get a rest at all. Maybe a month or two. Suddenly in February of 2002 Daire came back and he said, "It's on. We're up and running!" You know that he'd been in-volved in the planning of the station along with Denis O'Brien, Setanta and various people and the other shareholders of Newstalk 106. I have had no involvement in the business end of the station here. I'm just working as a journalist, as a hired hand. Daire said, "Well, we're starting", and I said, "How long do we have to train up for this kind of stuff?" He said, "You have a week!"

RG: I think that was pretty much the story all round, but any-way, go on.

DK: So we went down to this tiny little studio in Merrion Square and sort of pretended to be radio broadcasters for five days and they said, "It's all beginning next Monday", so that was it. That was how it all started here on Newstalk 106, 9 April 2002.

RG: And since then you've built up a fair old listenership on your lunchtime show and you've also not only been nominated, but walked away with a PPI Award. That must have been a crowning moment for you, was it?

DK: Now, Roger, the less said about that . . . we were very hon-oured, obviously, to receive awards but I've spent most of my life as a journalist giving out about journalists who've won prizes, so I'm not going to turn myself into a total and utter hypocrite now.

RG: You think journalism and pot hunting are not "at one"?

DK: I always thought when I was a newspaper journalist that extremely tedious feature writers had about a 20 times better chance of winning a journalism award than fellows or girls who went out and got really cracking news stories. They were the ones that I would have given the prizes to over the years.

RG: So the prevaricators at home on opinion and analysis were getting away with murder.

DK: Absolutely!

ℒara ℳarlowe

*A*s readers of **The Irish Times** *will know, Lara Marlowe is the
Paris-based Foreign Correspondent for that paper and has written
on international and European affairs, including covering wars in Iraq,
Afghanistan, Kosovo plus reporting trips to Lebanon, Syria, Iran and
Nigeria. She has also worked for a string of other publications and quality international newspapers including the* Financial Times, *the* International Herald Tribune *and the* San Francisco Chronicle. *Because
she is Paris-based this interview was conducted by phone — not always
an ideal situation, particularly in a lengthy conversation such as this.
However, I don't believe the quality of this interview was hampered by
not being face-to-face with Lara (a wish I have yet to realise). The interview was recorded the day after the death of Pope John Paul II.*

RG: Before we head into the personal interview, as it were, can you first give us an idea of the mood there in Paris since the death of the Pope yesterday evening?

LM: There's a sort of obsession about talking about anything else. Obviously there's been nothing else on the radio since Friday. I think there's a sense of relief that his suffering is over as well and many of the bishops who are being interviewed on television and radio are saying he fought very hard and were pleased that he is with the Lord and that he has made this passage. President Chirac made a speech last night after his death was announced. He'd sent a written communiqué and he's supposed to go on television today to make another short statement. France is of course known as the first daughter of the Church, although few French people are practising Catholics, but at times like this, their faith does come back to them.

RG: I'd like to move on if I may to talk about you. Take us back to the beginning — growing up, education and family and indeed your connections with Ireland.

LM: Well, I was born in California. My father died when I was small, my mother was a school teacher and I started learning French when I was ten years old and really took it up very seriously later on and that was a determining event. I came to Paris at the age of nineteen as a student and then went through graduate school in Britain and became a journalist when I finished.

RG: And was it your intention to become a journalist or did you drift into it like a lot of us?

LM: I sort of drifted into it. I had some other ideas. I considered becoming a lawyer or a banker or a diplomat but at the end of the day, journalism is what happened to me. It was the best choice, the one I'm most adapted to, I think, and it's the field in which I got a job when I finished graduate school.

RG: Your connections with Ireland — you say you were brought up in California — so what is the Irish connection apart from *The Irish Times*?

LM: Well I started coming to Ireland on holiday in the late eighties and when I was looking for freelance work, also in the late eighties, I contacted Paul Gillespie in the *Times* and did a lot of freelance work for the foreign desk and then I got a job with the *Financial Times* and stopped working for *The Irish Times*. In 1996 I was working for *Time* magazine but I wanted to leave it and work for a newspaper. I was on holiday in Ireland and I read a farewell piece by my predecessor Catherine Hone and I rang up Paul Gillespie and said: "Are you by any chance looking for a Paris correspondent?" He said "Yes" and that was the beginning of my second stay with *The Irish Times*.

RG: Your range of journalism is broad, but predominately foreign affairs. Would that be your favourite area?

LM: Yes, very much so. I enjoy covering France and French politics and culture but the interest in the Middle East is also very strong. I moved to Lebanon in 1988 and while I was there I covered the Arab world and the wars there and in former Yugoslavia and a couple of wars in Africa. But I would say my interest in the Middle East, the Arab world, Iran and Islam *per se* is very, very strong.

RG: When you were working in Beirut for the *Financial Times* and also *Time* magazine, what was it actually like there reporting in the late eighties and early nineties?

LM: They were of course the last years of the civil war which ended in 1990 but there were still more than a dozen killings as there were a lot of car bombs going off the first nine months that I was there. I lived in Beirut during the so-called war of liberation, ~~which meant that we were shelled every night. There were explo~~ sions going on all around. There was very little water or electricity but it was actually great training for everything that has followed. It prepared me for all the other wars that I've covered.

RG: But presumably it takes a high toll in the emotional stakes in terms of sheer terror. How do you cope with that?

LM: I think that I learned not to be afraid in advance. Obviously when something explodes nearby, you jump, your heart beats faster, but being in that experience there was a lot of violence at any moment and it was very unpredictable. You learned just to get on with your life during the quiet moments, to keep writing your story even if there were a lot of explosions going off around you, and that's a very useful experience. You learn to gauge the degree of danger — to know how close it is to you and when you do really need to get under the table or into the basement.

RG: Yes, but how do you actually gauge something like that? Well obviously through experience, but did you take any training in survival?

LM: No, no. You learn on the job. It's probably difficult for me in over . . . what, almost fifteen years now, maybe a bit more? But it's hard to remember the full terror, as you say, of those first bombardments. But there were times when I cried with fatigue. You do get very, very tired. But eventually fatigue sort of overcomes your fear and you can sleep through anything at the end of the day.

RG: More recently you covered the invasion of Iraq. In fact, I remember talking to you at length during that invasion on the late night show here on Newstalk 106. How did you cope with that as an assignment, as it was somewhat different, I would have thought — particularly the rights and wrongs of the allied invasion?

LM: Well the whole question of rights and wrongs you don't deal with in any war because, although there may be just wars, personally I'm someone who would think that war should be absolutely the last resort. In any event, even if you do feel that the war is in some way justified, as for example the previous Iraq war in 1991, when Iraq invaded Kuwait, there was obviously a good reason for that. But even there one always has feelings and there are always civilians killed and I always feel a sort of anger at people who kill civilians or injure them, as it very often seems unnecessary. The Iraq war in 2003 was probably the worst or most dangerous that I've covered because the sophistication of the weapons that the Americans use now is absolutely stunning — I mean the firepower that they have now. Whereas the Lebanon war in 1989 and the bombardments I was sitting through, you're talking about 120- to 240-millimetre artillery shells, and the Americans were dropping one-ton bombs and there's just no comparison of the noise, the sort of earthquake that it makes, the damage that it does and also its destruction of human lives. The sheer number of homes that are destroyed and also the wounds of the people I saw in the hospital were really quite appalling.

RG: What about the assimilation of information in a war zone like that? Sticking with Iraq, a lot of propaganda is obviously going to be dispensed by either side; how do you sift through that?

LM: I think you have to keep as much distance as possible from your minders, so to speak. It was fairly similar in Belgrade in 1999 during the NATO bombardment. You have to have a healthy degree of scepticism and you just tell it as you see it. I think in a way it's easier to do that when the host country, if you can call it that ... Saddam Hussein's regime or when they are so obviously dictators, and manipulators and propagandists, you're obviously not going to believe most of what they tell you and sometimes you can actually catch them out lying very blatantly and then you put that in your story. I think in a way it's more difficult if you are, say, an embedded journalist with American troops. Then there is a tendency on the part of the journalist to think, "Well, these are my people, they're like me, they would never lie to me, this is the gospel truth."

RG: How did you avoid "embedding" and what is the bias that, in your view, naturally comes from embedding?

LM: Well I avoided it in the most recent war because I was in Baghdad and I was on the receiving end of all that fire power. Actually, in the previous Iraq war I was there for *Time* magazine and I did participate in some of the media pools and one of the biggest propaganda coups that the US government carried off in the 1991 war was this oil spill. You remember that Saddam Hussein opened the oil wells and they portrayed it as a huge ecological disaster and there were all sorts of pictures of cuddly animals that were going to become extinct because of this oil spill. It emerged after the war that this was a CIA plant, basically, and there was no huge ecological disaster. In the Iraq war, the present Iraq war, there was no question of me being embedded because, as I say, I had an Iraqi visa and until the regime fell on 9 April 2003 I was under the surveillance, you might say, of Iraqi officials which was not pleasant but it was a whole different way of working.

RG: Was there a sense of protection?

LM:.   No. Not at all, not at all. You knew . . . in fact there were several western journalists who were under surveillance and who were actually arrested and thrown in jail because they ventured out of their hotel without permission or in the case of some photographers they were taking pictures from places where they weren't meant to. No, they weren't protecting us at all. On the contrary, they were harassing us. All of the journalists had satellite phones and for a very long time you weren't meant to be using them from your hotel rooms and they would send these sort of minders around, knocking on hotel room doors and bursting in through hotel room doors to see if people were cheating and using their satellite phones. There was one man who, during a bombardment, went around to the ground floor outside the hotel and looked up at the hotel balconies. He could see these satellite dishes on the balconies so he made notes of which rooms, counted the floors and the number of rooms and he'd then go and bust the journalists who were using their satellite phones. So there was this constant sort of harassment. They were also constantly shaking us down for money. The same man was taking thousands . . .

RG: When you say shaking us down for money, presumably you're talking physically there, so that therefore you were, if you like, accosted, no?

LM: Well it was all cloaked in the language of government bureaucracy that there was a fee for the use of the Information Ministry's Press Centre which of course was bombed out fairly early on and then we were working out of the hotel. There was a fee, basically, to work in Iraq. There was a fee to be allowed to use your own satellite phone. But when I did, the man in question would sort of grab you and he had a big list of who'd paid and who hadn't and I would keep my eyes out for him and every time I saw him in the quarters of the hotel or something I would just turn around and run as fast as I could in the other direction. So I avoided him for quite a number of days, knowing that the regime was about to fall and knowing that once it had fallen he would no longer be there asking me for money. I think I managed to save *The Irish Times* about $6,000 that way.

RG: Well I hope they rewarded you for that! But you've since been back to Iraq and apart from anything else, it must be highly dangerous now, particularly given the number of journalists who have been kidnapped. OK some have been released on foot of . . .

LM: . . . Yes, and some have been killed unfortunately . . .

RG: . . . Indeed, and some have been killed very dreadfully too. That must have been quite a worrying part of your life, returning there knowing the added dangers.

LM: It was, but again I think the experience helps a lot. I've learned over the years in these kind of situations to keep the lowest possible profile, to go round in a junky old car and just try not to be conspicuous in any way. I've also learned not to go to places where one is likely to be kidnapped. For example the Italian who was freed recently said she spent four hours in the refugee camp of people from Fallujah. Now several people have actually been kidnapped at that exact place or travelling there and sure enough she got kidnapped there and she said, after she was freed, "In retrospect, I should have only gone for twenty minutes or half an hour." You know these are very sort of basic elements of survival.

RG: You referred to driving around in a beaten-up car; you travel solo, or perhaps with a photographer and that's it, you have no protection at all, or do you have a guide?

LM: No, no, I work with just a driver and an interpreter. I don't work with a photographer; in fact sometimes I take my own photos for *The Irish Times*. Although in a difficult situation like that you don't want to be pulling at a camera. I think it's much more difficult for television cameramen and photographers . . .

RG: . . . given the nature of their equipment, they give themselves away.

LM: Exactly.

RG: Overall, what are your views on journalism in high-risk areas, in war areas? It has become more dangerous — well, it's always been dangerous, but it has intensified somewhat and an awful lot of journalists die, in fact I think it was 200 last year . . .

LM: Yes, but I think that was worldwide.

RG: Well that's what I mean.

LM: There were close to 60 killed in Iraq, most of them Arab or Iraqi journalists. I feel that the vocation of journalism is to cover the news. It is to get the story and imagine what our knowledge of, say, the Normandy landings, or the Second World War, or the Vietnam War would have been had journalists said at the time, "It's just too dangerous to cover." The fact is that many, many more journalists died covering those wars than have died in the Iraq war. I think our attitude towards it has changed, somehow, you know, we think our lives are more valuable than other people's. I mean, estimates are that perhaps 100,000 Iraqi civilians have died since the US invasion. Now I certainly wouldn't want to die and I wouldn't want any of my colleagues to die either, but I think in a situation like that, if journalists are going to cover these wars, it is going to be inevitable. What is really frightening now in Iraq is that journalists are singled out as potential hostages.

RG: I was just thinking of the Romanian journalists there at the moment, the three who were captured during the week. In a situation like that they are relying on a payoff in order to get out because there really is no other alternative, is there?

LM: No, no there's not. And certainly the governments who are often targeted — and this is the case with the Romanian government as well, which has a small contingent in Iraq — invariably the kidnappers are asking that the governments withdraw their troops from Iraq and no government has done that in those circumstances. Obviously about a dozen or so governments have pulled out of Iraq but not . . . with the exception of the Filipinos; I remember there were some Filipino hostages and they actually conceded. They said they'd pull all of their people out of Iraq. But certainly the British government for example or the US government are never going to give in to these kind of demands.

RG: And what are your views now on Iraq, in terms of it settling down or ostensibly settling down post-elections, etc.?

LM: Well it's been two months since the election and there's still no government, which is very bad news. I don't think that the results are known yet, but the violence continues. There are dozens of people getting killed every day and unfortunately, because it has become so dangerous, it is a very poorly covered conflict, but I think it is going to continue to be extremely unstable, extremely violent for certainly months and probably years to come.

RG: In the wake of covering wars, how do you, as a person, relax and chill after such assignments?

LM: Well after the Iraq war I had promised myself that if I survived, I would buy myself a baby grand piano and resume piano lessons which I'd stopped for about the last 25 or 30 years. And I promised myself that as I have some very dear friends in Florence — I promised that I would go to Florence for Maria's birthday, which I did. So you reward yourself with things like that. I think that was probably the worst exhaustion I'd ever experienced. I was there for six weeks, you know, through the invasion and the bombardment and then the aftermath . . . the looting and the fires all over the city and so on. It takes a bit of time, but you eventually sleep it off and I must say it is actually fantastic to come back to western Europe. I went to Ireland for a few days as well, just to sense that sort of security and the quiet and the peace of it and to realise what an immensely lucky person I am to live in the developed world, to live in countries that are not at war.

RG: Finally, having read your curriculum vitae, some years ago you wrote a biography of Robert Maxwell. What gave you that motivation to write about Captain Bob?

LM: Well actually I was approached by Tom Bower, the British journalist who was the main writer on it and I worked on the French version of it when a French publisher hired me to do it. Maxwell was a fascinating character. He was one of these sort of larger-than-life, totally unscrupulous, people and it was great fun.

Justine McCarthy

A specialist in feature writing, Justine McCarthy is an award-winning journalist with a diverse range of interests. She was chief features writer with the Irish Independent *and assistant editor with that paper and is a weekly columnist with the* Independent's Saturday *weekend supplement as well as continuing to write for the daily. She has also contributed to* The Observer, The Washington Post *and has worked in radio. She also wrote an acclaimed biography of President Mary McAleese entitled* The Outsider.

RG: You were in secondary school in Cork so obviously that's where you grew up. Can you tell us a bit about your family and growing up in Cork?

JM: I'm from County Cork, a town called Bandon, which is about 18 miles from the city, and I went to school in Cork city. I'm one of four daughters and my mother was the first feminist I ever met; her name is Bridie. My father died when we were very young and she was left with a typical country town business and she coped very well with it but her dictum in life for her four daughters was, "Have a career, no matter what you do", because she had found out the hard way how important it was.

RG: You mention that she was the first feminist you met, in fact your essay in the recent book *Quench Not the Light* actually deals with a lot of that. Explain it to the listeners, particularly in relation to her beliefs and attitudes to the Church.

JM: My mother is a very surprising woman because if you met her, you'd think she was a fragile little lady, very feminine, but she has a very well-developed feminist conscience. As a young woman, when she had her first baby, she went through what was called the "churching" ritual whereby new mothers had to be purified, cleansed in the Roman Catholic Church. She was so humiliated by the whole idea that what she had done was somehow dirty, in giving life to a child, that she swore that if she had other children she would not go through it again. Fortunately my father was of the same mind and for the subsequent three children she didn't go through the "churching" process.

RG: At what age did you decide you wanted to be a journalist because, certainly from reading your CV, you seem to have made that decision quite early in life. Is that right?

JM: I had made the decision that I wanted to write very early and it was only when a family friend called to the house when I was about fifteen and, as adults always do, he asked me what was I going to be when I grew up and I said "I don't know". He asked me, "What do you like doing?" and I said "I love writing" to which he said "Why don't you become a journalist?". I asked, "What do they do?" and then I realised it was like Lou Grant and I thought, yes, that's what I would love to do. Print journalism is where it's at for me. I would never want to be away from it. It's not just the writing, which is absolutely foremost for me, but the whole tradition, the whole atmosphere of print journalism is addictive.

RG: You have worked in radio but you weren't tempted to go into broadcasting?

JM: I wouldn't trust myself to be a broadcast journalist by profession. I think I wouldn't have that ability to live on my nerves and to jump into the breach when guests like myself suddenly get a mental block. I have seen professional broadcasters doing that and I'm full of admiration. But no, I wouldn't. I enjoy doing the odd bit. It's nice to keep in that side of journalism because it is such a hugely relevant field of journalism today. I think writing gives you much more time to be reflective and more space. Funnily enough, something I've realised because of working in radio is that you fit far more into the written word than into the spoken word.

RG: Well you do, yes, and the other thing you've got to do is hurry through a story because you've got to move onto the next one fairly quickly and there is that frenetic atmosphere to it. But how did you actually start? You went to Rathmines, didn't you?

JM: I did, yes, at a time when there was no alternative really. It was a two-year course in the College of Commerce in Rathmines. You had to have two honours in your Leaving Certificate, preferably one in English and one in another language, Irish or French. The two-year course consisted of nine subjects, two of which were shorthand and typing. They were really the two that we needed. The other seven you could have dispensed with — newspaper law and economics, etc.

RG: Well of course shorthand is an invaluable skill to acquire, but mostly dropped now in journalism courses.

JM: I notice younger people, coming in now, don't have short-hand and it baffles me how they cope. I just don't understand how you could do the job without it.

RG: They're relying on Dictaphones or whatever. So what was your first break after you left Rathmines?

JM: I got a very glamorous job with a magazine called *Commercial Transport* which was based in Rathcoole, County Dublin. It was a monthly magazine with two journalists working on it, the editor and myself. Unfortunately, the editor had a very strong interest in horses, so very seldom appeared in the office which meant that for my very first job, at the age of 19, I was producing the magazine. The highlight of my two years there was a press trip to Leighton Buzzard, in Bedfordshire, to test drive a forklift truck. But I only pretended to test drive it because the demonstrator was actually working the pedals and I was turning the steering wheel!

RG: Really, and that qualified as being a test drive!?

JM: It did indeed!

RG: What an extraordinary magazine to get a break on, though, *Commercial Transport*! Not a subject, I would have thought, that you were interested in, or were you?

JM: I knew nothing about it and knew just as little two years later when I left. At that time there were very few jobs in Irish journalism. If you think back, this was the end of the seventies, 1979, when I left college. There was no independent radio. We did have the *Irish Press* but we didn't have any Irish editions of the British newspapers. We were literally stuck with the *Press*, the *Irish Independent* and *The Irish Times* and, of course, the *Examiner* in Cork. So most people of my age would have gone into either the provincial papers, if they were very good and very lucky, or into the trade magazines.

RG: And then you played a major part in the *Irish Independent* over the years as a journalist, but you were also with *Aspect* magazine. Can you remind us of *Aspect* magazine?

JM: *Aspect* started with great ambitions to be the new *Magill*. *Magill*, as we remember it, was still going at the time and *Aspect* was to be an investigative, pioneering, current affairs magazine. It was founded by Kevin Kelly, of *Image* fame, and a man called John O'Neill who had worked with him in a business magazine.

RG: John O'Neill used to run *Irish Business* magazine.

JM: That's right and *Aspect* was published out of Kevin Kelly's offices in Dun Laoghaire. There were three reporters and an editor and I think within six months all of us had been sacked. Money became the priority. There was no money. It limped on for some time afterwards and then, as many do, it just disappeared.

RG: Now bring us on to your association with the Independent Group. How did you start there?

JM: I had no emotional attachment to the *Independent* whatso-ever. Being from Cork, I had grown up on the *Examiner*. But when things were winding down in *Aspect* and it was obvious that it wasn't going to survive, an ad appeared in the papers for a fea-tures writer for the *Irish Independent* and I duly applied and didn't get the job. But the features editor, Michael Brophy, who's now with the *Sunday World*, rang me up and said that he was inter-ested in meeting me with a view to doing some freelance work. I met him and the very first thing I wrote for the *Independent* was a series of features on society hostesses in Dublin. These were the wives of wealthy company executives who did a lot of entertaining at home for their husbands' businesses and it actually was quite controversial.

RG: In what way?

JM: Well one woman in particular had been very indiscreet in talking about the amount of money that she spent on petit fours in Brown Thomas's food department and would send the bill into the company on Monday morning! I never looked back after that and I stayed with the *Indo*, I love the place. I think it's a real gritty paper.

RG: So you started off as a freelance features writer and when did you become staff?

JM: Two years later.

RG: And was that into the newsroom or did you stick with features?

JM: I was staffed as a features writer. During the time freelancing I would have done newsroom shifts as well and it was around that time that Vinnie Doyle, the editor of the *Independent*, was starting to develop the colour writing side of news reporting. There was a woman freelancing at the same time called Liz Ryan and we were the only two freelancing in features. Liz was a wonderful colour writer and the two of us made a fortune freelancing as colour writers and feature writers. The problem when I got staffed was that I had far more time than I had as a freelance, but far less money to go to the shops and spend!

RG: But you had a depth of experience as a features writer and as a colour writer for news background. What are your favoured areas of journalism as you have had a wide range of experience?

JM: Features writing, definitely, because you have the space and the time to learn as much as you can about a subject, to explore different aspects and to look back as well. When you're doing news, you're running with a story and there's no time to actually put it in context whereas with a feature that's probably the biggest advantage . . .

RG: . . . is that you can stand back from it and actually analyse it in greater depth. Moving on, you've covered a lot of stories from the States over the years and also more recently you did the All First Bank story. What are your thoughts now on covering that one?

JM: The difference in the way they do things in the United States and here was interesting. There is more transparency in corporate America than there is in corporate Ireland. Having said that, it was fundamentally an Irish bank, so I was dealing with Irish people. But the financial authorities there in Baltimore, I found them more amenable and far less frightened of providing information. That was wonderful. I wish it could be like that all the time.

RG: Do you mean in terms of whistle-blowing or officials not being protective of what they say?

JM: In terms of returning calls and answering the questions they're asked and providing simple information.

RG: Which, you're saying, wouldn't necessarily be forthcoming in this country?

JM: No. I think it's changing very, very slowly. There is still an attitude in the public service here that information is something that should be kept among a very small coterie of people and not shared, which is only bound to make people far more suspicious and dig deeper.

RG: And has the Freedom of Information Act not helped that?

JM: I have found the Freedom of Information Act virtually useless.

RG: Yes, well this is what a lot of people say simply because people are writing or putting down memos with the FOI in the back of their minds knowing that the information can be accessed.

JM: That's right.

RG: So you actually think it has created a more secretive society?

JM: I think in a way it has because it's given the impression that there is more accountability and that we're all far more open about everything. Whereas in fact I think a lot of the time it amounts to a cosmetic exercise. It's a very onerous, time-consuming process in the first place. You have to go from A to B and C and if that doesn't work out you end up at Z and then you have to appeal the decision. It all costs a lot of money and by the time the appeal has progressed — this happened to me recently — I had just lost the energy to keep fighting it.

RG: But that's the idea of it, obfuscation in the hope that you'll go away and making it as difficult as possible to access, which is quite appalling and I presume something that the Ombudsman will be challenging or she certainly should be with her background. Now, you also covered Somalia when President Robinson visited that country.

JM: Something that I'm very grateful to have done but it was horrendous at the time. I remember the day we arrived in Somalia, we'd come up from Kenya in very small chartered planes in dribs and drabs. The travelling party with the President had met at a rendezvous and I was sitting on a bus, waiting for everybody to get on the bus so that we could go to wherever we were going and I was looking out the window at a man lying on the ground, dying, and there was nothing I could do.

RG: Difficult to stand back in that instance. How did you cope?

JM: I remember Vincent Browne had been there for a week or two before the rest of us arrived and he was on the bus with me and I said, "We've got to do something for that man. We can't sit here watching him dying" and he said, "You're just going to have to accept it". He said that he had felt exactly the same when he arrived and that you have to accept that there is just nothing that you can do to save the individual life but there were things we could do in our jobs to alert people to what was happening.

RG: And presumably that experience has stayed with you?

JM: It has. The overpowering thing that hit me when I arrived in the country was the smell and for quite a while I couldn't figure out what this smell was. It was a smell I had never smelt in my life. It took me a while to realise that it was the smell of rotting humanity. It's very hard to come back to a so-called first world country after that experience and go out to dinner in a restaurant or even to hear yourself saying, "I'm starving, I'm going for something to eat."

RG: Has a sense of guilt stayed with you?

JM: A sense of guilt, yes, and of course it has faded over time and now and again you see the images on television and it's a reminder of what the reality is for a lot of people. I remember going down to Kenya, to Nairobi, straight from Mogadishu and Mary

Robinson gave her international press conference where she cried and I remember sitting in the room with this feeling that everybody in the room was afraid to move. This was such an extraordinary moment that a woman like this, who a lot of us would have thought was cold, very aloof and very reserved, was sitting there with tears running down her face and I think some of the journalists who had been there with her and saw what she'd seen, had tears in their eyes as well.

RG: I can only imagine. Onto another story you covered: Gibraltar and the killings there of the IRA Three. That must have been a difficult one to cover?

JM: You know in a funny way it wasn't because if you remember, the witnesses in Gibraltar, people like the woman Carmen Pruetta who had seen the killings from her apartment window . . .

RG: . . . this is the woman who was discredited because she had had a professional life as a prostitute?

JM: That's right, yes, and there was a lawyer called, I think his name was Stephen Bullock, who had actually got his law degree in Trinity College even though he had no Irish connection and there were other witnesses as well. These people had such integrity, they were so determined to tell the truth about what they had seen, that they made life very easy for people like me. I mean, I was no more than a note-taker, really. I remember going up to Carmen Pruetta's apartment and standing on the balcony which had been her vantage point when the three IRA people had been shot and seeing how clearly she would have viewed the events that day. The woman was just so impressive, I knew she wasn't lying and she swore, when I interviewed her — this was quite soon after the killings — that no matter what was written about her or what was said about her, that she would go into a court of law and tell the truth exactly as she saw it.

RG: Let's move on to a totally different subject: *The Outsider*, your biography of President McAleese. You took six months off from the *Independent* to write that so what was your motivation there? Was it your idea to write the book; presumably it was?

JM: No, actually it wasn't. I had been in Belgium for the opening of the Peace Park commemorating the Irish involvement in the war. It had been opened by Mary McAleese and the Queen of England and after that a publisher, John O'Connor of Blackwater Press, rang me up and asked me would I be interested in writing a biography of Mary McAleese and, as soon as he said it, I was very excited about it. I had followed Mary Robinson very closely and I remember the jubilation when she was elected and I had read the biographies of Mary Robinson and had felt very enthusiastic about that whole thing. So I didn't ask Mary McAleese for co-operation when I went to do the book. I didn't want it because, I suppose, the journalist in me would prefer to be independent rather than to be ghost-writing her story.

RG: Finally, women in journalism generally — and I think you would probably have to go back to *The Guardian* in the late sixties and early seventies, when Jill Tweedie and Polly Toynbee were there — up until that point, women journalists were, to a degree, ghettoised, were they not? How do you think this has improved over the last twenty or so years?

JM: Very slowly and in need of major change still. By coincidence, I was reading a piece by Polly Toynbee in, I think it was the *Media Guardian*, where she was talking about setting up a group of women journalists in London — this is as recently as 1991 I think — who supported each other and encouraged each other because nowhere is the glass ceiling as obvious as it is in the media. When I became a journalist there were fairly few women. If you went out on a news story, for instance, it would mostly be men. I'd say now it is at least 50–50 and very often there are far more women reporters than male reporters. But if you look at the management structure, it is practically, I suppose, 90 per cent men in Ireland, much more so than in Britain.

RG: Well, certainly at editor level, but then of course we've got Geraldine Kennedy editing *The Irish Times* and we have Noreen Hegarty now as well editing the *Tribune*.

JM: Yes, but isn't it sad that we can only name two women?

RG: At that level, yes. So you feel that women are still being, well, not ghettoised, but restricted, or feel that you are, perhaps, being restricted in advancing up the editorial chain?

JM: Not personally, I think, because I've been there so long, but I do think it is harder for women to get into decision-making roles in journalism and I think that's very bad for the readers and the listeners because I don't think there's a very balanced view being put across. For instance, at the moment, I detect a certain fashion in Irish journalism for "laddishness". I would even go so far as to say that you might have a bit of it in this station; you know, you have the Eamon Dunphys and the George Hooks. I'm not saying they're laddish but there is a certain sort of sporting, male perspective. We have it in the *Independent*. I see it in the magazines and I think if more women were having an input into how matters are covered and how they are analysed it would be better for everybody.

$\mathcal{C}$aroline $\mathcal{M}$orahan

$\mathcal{S}$artorial elegance is not something I get hung up about but no doubt I'm in a minority. The rag trade is big business, driving the fads and trends of fashion for both male and female, and it engulfs the media. Women's fashion magazines turn great stashes of cash everyday, propagating what is a "must have" for the female wardrobe. Some say it's a manipulative industry with dire psychological implications for its victims. Others eschew such opinion and wallow in the glamour of the latest little black number from the house of Versace. Caroline Morahan would come under the latter category as she's lived fashion for the last few years and has written about it, as well as being one of two front women on RTÉ's highly successful programme Off the Rails.

RG: You're a graduate of DCU in Communications. What attracted you to that degree?

CM: Well before I begin on that I've yet to own a little black Versace number, I'm sad to report, but I'm working on it! But what attracted me to Communications, after I did my Leaving Cert, was my interest in the media. I was interested in lots of different aspects of it and I wanted to delve into them all because I didn't know specifically what I wanted. So I thought it would be a nice broad degree which would give me a flavour of lots of different things and it would give me an opportunity to breathe and develop and decide what I wanted because at that age, 17, you don't know what your career plan is.

RG: And what did the degree encompass?

CM: Well all areas of media. I focused on photography in which I took a fashion slant. I did my thesis in photography and it was very much fashion-driven. I also studied film, the public relations element of media, the money behind current trends in film, creative writing and the more sociological aspects of things as well. So it really was perfect for me; the things I was interested in I drank in, and the things I wasn't, as the years went on, I was able pare down and focus on the direction I wanted to go.

RG: And you geared yourself towards journalism, didn't you?

CM: Well when I finished my degree I went travelling for a number of months and when I came back I wanted to work in television. The reason for that was, during my second year in college, I'd been working in a promotions company just to get through college and it was very good money for very little time. I would do the horrible 7.00 am jobs of giving out flyers and that kind of thing.

RG: That must be soul-destroying, is it?

CM: Well I have to say it was difficult getting up quite early and being in pollutant fumes. But I enjoyed smiling at people and while I was doing that they spotted that I could act so they had me doing a few character things. It was through that that another guy, who was a comedian working in the agency, was asked to do a pilot for a television programme. The producer needed a female co-presenter and he knew no one, but he'd met me, we'd spoken once or twice and he thought that I'd be good for it. So I was literally thrown into this television set, live! But it was a pilot and nothing actually came of it.

RG: What sort of a programme was it?

CM: It was a music programme — there isn't anything like it on television. It was following Irish bands, doing profiles on them, their fans and generating a fan base for them. The way it works now is it's a sub-culture but this was attempting to let other people latch onto things and really build support around bands. One of the people we interviewed was Jack L and his band. At that stage people didn't know who he was and he has since become quite prominent and he's a spectacular performer. So I was literally handed a microphone and I had to interview him and his band and "spot" interview fans outside. I was physically ill before doing it because I thought, "I'm not going to be able to do this", you know, all the usual insecurities that you have. As soon as the red light went on I just loved it, was exhilarated by it, loved the challenge and knew that this is what I wanted to do. When I'd left college I made every attempt to get into presenting but I was just met with slamming doors. At the time TV3 was fledgling but they said that they had everyone they needed. They said that they'd keep me on file. The pilot got down to one of the last few choices pitched to RTÉ but they decided not to go with it and they didn't need any young, female presenters. I was hitting my head against a brick wall. So I lost my path for a couple of years and I just needed to earn money so I was temping and working in finance. I say I lost my path because I'm not a numbers whiz and here I was working with tens of millions of euro and dollars and all the rest. It's not where my skills are, but it was vital for me because it gave me a professionalism that I didn't have. I was out working in the real world, having to conduct meetings and all of that — essential learning.

RG: So then journalism came your way. You were writing for the *Evening Herald*; were you drawn more to journalism than presenting?

CM: I'm the very same now as I was then. I've lots of different things on the go at all times and I think in this day and age you have to be that way. I mean the idea of walking into one job and staying there for life doesn't really exist. It became quite apparent when I was in this financial job as a temp, which turned into a year or nearly two years. It just hit me one day and I realised I wasn't using any of my real talents. I knew I'd learned all I could and I had studied financial law, accountancy and share transfer when I was there because that was the business I was in and I wanted to understand it. Then, having successfully got all the different qualifications, I knew it wasn't for me. So, Roger, I just made a list of the things I wanted to do. Television presenting and journalism were on the list and I just made my way through the list and that's literally how I did it.

RG: You made a very valid point in relation to the lack of permanency in jobs but also the other aspect of it, which is multi-skilling. Presumably, going back to your Communications degree, that would have given you a fair idea of the various facets of the media?

CM: In terms of my Communications degree, and I'm sure this kind of thing happens a lot through life where you don't really appreciate it to the same extent that you should at the time. I enjoyed my degree thoroughly, but I could have got more from it. I could have been more involved in different things but I did just what I had to do . . .

RG: . . . to get by, just like many students?

CM: Exactly, each year I would join every society going and then I'd go to one meeting and that would be it. I approached the *Evening Herald*, because I'd decided I wanted to write about fashion. I didn't decide I wanted to write about fashion just for the *Herald*. I'd looked at lots of different publications and what was going on at the time. It was by chance that P.J. Gibbons, now the editor of *Social and Personal* magazine, wrote for the *Examiner* and my father writes for the *Examiner*. So he said to P.J. that Caroline really wants to write about fashion, but that was P.J.'s niche and so he asked if there was anything he could suggest. P.J. mentioned that he knew that the fashion editor of the *Herald* had just moved to Scotland, so there was an opening there and that's why I made a five-pronged attack on the *Herald* and approached them.

RG: As their fashion correspondent? Because you wouldn't have had any proof that you knew anything about fashion.

CM: Absolutely! Before I approached them I had to have an article or work to show them, which I didn't have. So I contacted every PR company in Dublin, said that I was a freelance journalist specialising in fashion, and asked them to put me on their lists. Immediately I was aware of what was happening. I just turned up at events to find out who was who and quite quickly I built up a network. I was getting all the information and I was no longer on the outside looking in. I knew what was happening. That took a lot of work and I wasn't being paid. Then there was the annual Futura Fair in the RDS, which is where all the buyers examine the trends for the coming seasons. I went along to that just to look for a story. I came across a group of girls who were my age or younger, in their very early twenties, with their own label. I thought, "That's got to be a story", because fashion in Ireland is notoriously difficult. John Rocha has gone under, I think, two or three times in his 25-year career and for these girls to be going for it was admirable and worthy of an interview. I interviewed them, but I was such a novice I walked off and realised I hadn't checked the spelling of their names and had to go back to them about three times because I'd forgotten crucial bits of information. But they were at the same stage themselves.

RG: But it worked and you got it into the *Herald*.

CM: I put it into the *Herald* and they literally rang me straight away, asked for a picture and told me to set it up. And the relationship was born from there on.

RG: Another aspect of your career is acting. You've done quite a bit and you're well known for your role in *Fair City*. Will you tell me about that?

CM: Well, just to get back to the notion that I'm well known . . . I remember last year I got a call from the programme *Blizzard of Od* where Colin Murphy, a comedian, literally takes the "mick" out of anyone and everyone. They were hoping to do that with me and the researcher asked if they could use one of my show reels or a pilot I'd done. I had nothing to give them so I said there's a pretty embarrassing piece of footage in the archives from when I was in *Fair City* and the researcher nearly fell off the chair, she was so delighted with it. So off she went and mortified me and Colin got a good bit of mileage out of it, but I wouldn't say I'm well known. It's about ten years ago or more, I was fifteen at the time and I'd been in the Betty Ann Norton School of acting from the age of four, but not with a view to a career in acting.

RG: But had you done amateur dramatics?

CM: Well we'd put on regular productions every week. She really pushed us and when I look back on it now the kind of education I got from her and from her husband Michael on aspects of language, drama, posture, was wonderful. It really was an education in the real sense of the word, leading you into all this knowledge. It was a phenomenal experience; it wasn't just tap-dancing with rosy cheeks . . .

RG: . . . and ringlets!

CM: Exactly that, but there were no ringlets! I had been acting from a very young age, but my mother always said to me that an actor's life is the hardest because you could be working one week and then not working for six. She said, "If you want to do it we're a hundred per cent behind you but you have to know that it's what you want to do." So with those words echoing in my mind I never felt that I had the gift to do it and make a go of it. I would say it's a dormant passion of mine. When I go to different award ceremonies and things where film is involved, I look longingly at various actors and I am aware that it's such an incredible achievement to have a film career, but I don't feel confident in my abilities in that department to really go for it. That's why I only do things that I think I'm very good at. If I don't feel I'm very good at it, I just leave it.

RG: So you've left the acting behind then?

CM: I kind of have. I'd love to, behind closed doors, do another course and play with it and enjoy it as opposed to making it a career. It really is phenomenal, like reading a great book. You're transported and it's comparable to returning to that child-like state where your imagination is boundless and endless. It's very fulfilling from that point of view.

RG: Moving on to *Off the Rails*, how did that come about for you?

CM: *Off the Rails* is amazing and I pinch myself twice daily. It really came about because of my big break in television, a quiz show called *The Fame Game*. My sister was doing an MA in film in Aungier Street and saw an RTÉ poster there advertising for a TV presenter to front a new quiz show. She told me to go for it because at that stage my journalism career was really taking off. The *Evening Herald* had given me my own column and things were chugging along quite nicely. So I decided to give it a shot. It was Adare Productions, based out in Monkstown, who are responsible for Hector's programmes, a very, very creative team. I discovered they were actually going to be filming the auditions, *Pop Star* style, before the contest, and I could see the potential for really embarrassing editing. So I decided to give it a miss because I didn't really want to risk jeopardising the career that I'd poured my blood, sweat, tears and the rest of it into. I didn't want my peers to say, "Here's some idiot who wants to have her face splashed across TV screens."

RG: This is the confidence thing again, is it, or the lack of it?

CM: No, I'd count myself as being a very confident person when I know I'm good at something. I know you should never really care too much about what people think. But that was my fear — that my colleagues would think I was fame-hungry, which was not what I'd wanted.

RG: And how many were auditioning?

CM: Two thousand auditioned and we were whittled from that number down to 30. I knew I was going to be in that 30 because I was very confident and very relaxed. I knew what I was doing and I presented well. I'd planned my audition with military precision. But every time my name was called as a finalist I was shocked and I couldn't believe it. On the eve of the final audition when we were down to five, I said to my mum that I wasn't too sure if I wanted this. I wasn't really sure if I wanted people to recognise me from doing a TV programme because my experience from *Fair City* had been quite negative. People really did recognise me and would shout things at me from passing cars.

RG: But that was because of the character presumably, Barbara Cleary?

CM: Well, yes, she was less than savoury, we'll say. But being recognised full stop, no matter whether it's in a positive light or a negative light, has to be something you're ready to deal with because when you're out with your friends or whatever it's not pleasant.

RG: But presumably you overcame that once you started *Off the Rails*?

CM: My mum told me, "You're older now, you've developed and you don't have that soft underbelly of a 15-year old." And all the things she said were right because I don't define how I feel by what people say about me. Some people will like the work I do and some won't. I know I do a good job so I don't really listen too much to what people say.

RG: So between your presenting work and the fashion journalism, what have you gleaned or what are your views on the industry generally?

CM: Well having started in journalism and reading everything about fashion constantly, looking at trends and trying to get to grips with names . . . I really admire Constance Harrison in the *Sunday Independent* for her sheer expanse of knowledge. The woman is a walking fashion encyclopaedia. . . . But the thing that has overwhelmed me is the cyclical nature of fashion. We've all known that flares were in in the seventies and they came back into fashion for a brief spell in the nineties and black and white was fashionable in the sixties and then it re-appeared in 2002 or whatever. The fact that it is so precisely repeated and fashion editors the world over sit in their production meetings every month have to ask how they'll make this different again.

RG: The industry is very much designer-driven but equally nothing new really comes up. It's really just repetition of themes, is that what you're saying?

CM: There are obviously new things, different ways of doing things that are quite inventive. But the cycle still repeats itself and it's very closely tied into economic shifts. If you just think about the eighties and the masculinity of the female suit with the shoulder pads saying, "We've got money and now we're going to show it", versus when things aren't going so well and everyone pares it down and goes back to the muted tones. It's really interesting from that point of view and new things do emerge. But the thing that first struck me, when I started writing my fashion features for the *Herald*, I was talking about tweed and the big thing at the time was Madonna's emergence as lady of the manor, that whole Burberry tweed fascination. Last autumn, tweed was the big story and we've done it before, but it'll creep in there at some stage in the future, so never throw anything out because three years down the line you'll be looking for it.

RG: Finally, do you think the fashion industry is exploitative?

CM: Yes, I do, absolutely. The fashion industry can make you feel great and it can make you feel awful. People need to know how to treat it. As a teenager myself, flicking through magazines was not a pleasant experience. I didn't realise that the bodies I was looking at were computer-generated and that you were looking at someone's legs that had been stretched by five inches in post-production. So from that point of view women need to realise that they're not looking at a real image. If I'm doing a photo shoot I have a trained make-up artist doing my make-up, I've got the best hairdresser and they spend up to two hours tweaking.

RG: But it's not just computer manipulation of images, because if you go back to the sixties, models like Twiggy, for example, were stick thin and they clearly wanted to get models who were just skin and bone.

CM: You're talking about the slim thing rather than the artificial image. Well, the slim thing breaks my heart because it's a chicken-and-egg situation. You want to say to the model-booking agents, "Why are you booking models who look like they're going to fall down dead?" It goes back to the designers because the designers' samples come in size small so they need to go on a small body. Models are supposed to be clothes horses but they've now become the movie-stars of old in our culture and we're confusing the thing. A model is a model because she's that shape and the rest of us aren't models because were not that shape and never can be. Lots of people want to be like that and they don't understand that these girls watch absolutely everything that they eat, everything!

Joe Mulholland

*F*rom the late seventies until the late nineties, Joe Mulholland was
one of the principal players in senior management within RTÉ. He
took early retirement from RTÉ having spent the greater part of his
working life with the state broadcaster, in many roles from producer, to
head of news and current affairs and on to senior management. He is
also a former chairman of the news division of the European Broadcasting Union (EBU). He's acknowledged as being a leading broadcast professional who has contributed to the shaping of broadcasting structure
and policy in Ireland, Europe and further afield.

RG: Can you take us back to the beginning, where you were
brought up, schooling and university?

JM: I was born and brought up in Donegal in a place called the
twin towns of Stranolar and Ballybofey and they straddle the Finn

River and they're called, for whatever reason, the twin towns. I went to school there, managed to get a scholarship when I was 14 to the local day school, secondary school, which enabled me to get a second-level education, which normally I wouldn't have got because we came from a very modest background. My father worked for most of his life in England and Scotland, as many Donegal men did at the time. So that enabled me to go on and do my Leaving Certificate and then I had to go to England. Third-level education was out of the question for people like myself and for families like ourselves, so I went to England and managed to get a third-level education there and from there I went on to France and furthered my studies.

RG: You went to France and did a doctorate there, if I'm right?

JM: I did a degree in French studies first of all, grammar and all the rest of it, and literature, a great experience, particularly because it was from 1964 to '68, so I straddled that whole '68 period in France. Then I went on to do a doctorate in medieval theatre, on the mystery plays, nothing to do with what I was to do, nothing to do with broadcasting.

RG: It must have been a help nonetheless. But at that stage had you notions of going into broadcasting or was your interest in theatre production?

JM: Well I had begun to get interested in theatre by putting on plays with my students in Nancy in France, that's where I was teaching and, of course, I was teaching part time and going to the university. So I began putting on Irish plays in French with my students; for example, Synge's *Playboy of the Western World* and then plays by O'Casey such as *Shadow of a Gunman*. I suppose I was inclined to the arts in any case and I had done a little bit of amateur theatre when I was growing up in Donegal. The amateur theatre movement, as you know, has been terrific in this country.

Then I got interested in photography but it was really by chance. I bumped into two Irish students at the University of Nancy, who were there for a year. They said, "My goodness, you must take an interest in television, RTÉ is developing and they're sometimes looking for producers."

RG: But at that stage, apart from your interest in theatre, were you considering an academic career?

JM: I was, yes, very much so and in fact when I was doing the interviews to become a trainee producer in RTÉ, I came back to Dublin for those, I had got a job offer in the University of Khartoum, in the Sudan, as a lecturer in French but that didn't appeal to me that much and, indeed, it had always been my ambition to come back to Ireland.

RG: So you did that just after RTÉ had set up the television end of things in 1963?

JM: I went to France from England where I had trained as a teacher and I went to France in '64 and I came back to Ireland to join RTÉ in January 1970. So it was well established. But interestingly our producer/director course was the first course that had been organised by RTÉ itself, within RTÉ. Previous to that, trainee producers were sent to the BBC or wherever. So this was the first, fully fledged in-house RTÉ training course.

RG: Which sadly they've now given up, or certainly they've given up the training studio?

JM: Eh, well that's another day's work.

RG: I don't mean they've given up training!

JM: Well the training studios are no more, which is something of a pity.

RG: So what attracted you to the area of broadcasting then, apart from the two Irish students suggesting that you apply? Were you drawn to the idea of broadcasting and being a producer?

JM: To my mind, in teaching and broadcasting there is very much a common strand in that you have something to impart and you want to impart it. Of course the difference with broadcasting is you get to a much wider audience. In the case of broadcasting and because of my background, the academic background and because of my own personality and my teaching, I've always taken a very "teaching" kind of view of broadcasting and I believe it to be very powerful in that regard.

RG: You mean in terms of imparting information?

JM: Exactly and in terms of education, educating and influencing people's opinions and influencing minds. Unfortunately broadcasting is tending to become something different.

RG: Sure and I wanted to get on to that because what you're basically saying is that you admire its facility and its ability to entertain and inform, in true Reithian values, is that it?

JM: Absolutely and I would be an absolute disciple of Reith, the BBC boss, and anything he did or said about broadcasting, I would concur with.

RG: But of course the map has changed very considerably since Reith.

JM: Very much so.

RG: But just sticking with RTÉ and Reithian values, it could be argued and in fact it is argued quite frequently, that things such as

Desperate Housewives or *Joey* which RTÉ 2 are now putting out, do not fall into that remit in my book and yours, if my guess is right.

JM: Well they certainly don't fall into it in my book either. I suppose broadcasters will argue and I have argued it myself, that you need a bit of everything and you need to be satisfying a mass audience and, if you're not, the danger is you become irrelevant and that has been the philosophy that has guided myself and others. But I do tend to see it as going too far in the direction of that kind of television.

RG: It's obviously ratings-driven.

JM: *Big Brother* and these things would have no interest for me whatsoever. That is not to say that one wouldn't, as controller or director of television, put them on, because, as I say there are huge pressures on people who are running television and particularly public television, in that they are pulled between these two things.

RG: And particularly in the situation we have here with RTÉ. They have the dual funding, the licence fee and the advertising revenue and of course the two, in many ways, conflict with each other, particularly the advertising end of things where the emphasis is on audience ratings.

JM: Correct, although in my time, we were overly dependent on commercial revenue, on advertising, because the licence fee was in the region, as you know, of 70 punts then. It has now more than doubled, so that has eased that situation and I think, therefore, it behoves the national broadcaster to keep a balance between the two. Or even to err, maybe, on the side of more serious broadcasting, without being boring.

RG: But there's plenty of room for both entertaining and quality documentary, for example, or current affairs programmes, which are still very much the backbone of RTÉ and I think you would agree with that. You were involved in that area from the seventies, presumably?

JM: Well true, I worked in the old *Seven Days* and went on to set up *Today Tonight*. I was editor of that for six years. I've always believed that the backbone of television schedules of any organisation, and certainly of a public service broadcaster, is news and current affairs. Particularly in this country where there is such an appetite and where people are informed and wish to be informed and I'm very glad to say that the news department, which I ran, and the news division and current affairs which I was also involved in, are very strong in RTÉ and hold a central place in the schedule and long may it continue.

RG: Now you've said that for the most part RTÉ's news service is good and people do acknowledge that. There's one area that RTÉ occasionally gets blamed for and certainly in the seventies, it was blamed for a lean one way or the other. Do you take that criticism as being unfair? I'm going back to the era when there was, ostensibly, a very left-wing element within the RTÉ newsroom.

JM: Well this has been said over the years under various governments and in various programmes and it probably has been said more in terms of current affairs than in news. And of course the old *Seven Days* under Muiris Mac Conghail, for example, was supposed to be totally dominated by the Labour Party or people like David Thornley, who was a presenter on it. But these were people of huge professionalism, of huge intellectual ability and just because, maybe, they were asking questions that the government of the day didn't like, then it's so easy to brand a programme or a group of people as left-wing. And of course that also applies in the UK where even the present Labour government will see the BBC as a nest of subversives. There is inevitably, I suppose, a continual tension between the two. I don't think that any programme in RTÉ was overly left-wing.

RG: Another aspect of it was republican sympathy as well which at the time, again in the seventies, was, I won't say constantly being reported, but it was certainly mentioned and various commentators in the print media would have alluded to it.

JM: I think there were times when, particularly at the beginning of the troubles in the North, people were swept along by a huge wave of emotionalism and of sympathy with the nationalist cause. I suppose this ultimately led to Section 31 and all of what followed.

RG: Which would have inflamed the situation.

JM: Yes, but I suppose at the time it was natural and we were all terribly moved and shaken by things like Bloody Sunday and indeed earlier, by the attacks on nationalist areas. So there is no doubt that in those situations there have been some lapses. But I think that overall RTÉ has provided an incredibly professional service and there's a lot of integrity in its news and current affairs and it has struck, in the main, the right balance.

RG: You've seen many governments or administrations come and go over the years. What was the relationship like with the various governments under which you would have served in RTÉ, and by that I mean the relationship in terms of wanting to espouse an ideology of one sort or another. So what sort of pressures came from government or from the GIS?

JM: Never much pressure, I have to say, in my own experience. Obviously there were tensions from time to time. Perhaps there was a feeling that the other side was being favoured or that the programme was pursuing a certain agenda. That surfaced from time to time and you might have got the odd phone call from the Government Information Office, the Director of the Government Information Office and so on. And from time to time from a politician — but very, very seldom and very rarely. I think politicians were wise enough to understand that within RTÉ there were enough checks and balances and that journalists, in the main, were of a professional standard and probably they reckoned it was dangerous as well to interfere or be seen to be interfering or to be seen to be trying to influence.

RG: Because it obviously harms the democratic process and is seen to do that as well. Now, let's get back to you and your working days in RTÉ. You moved from originally being a producer, then to editor and then to head of news and finally you moved into senior management. Did you enjoy that move or would you have preferred to have stayed on the floor, as it were?

JM: I enjoyed producing, particularly documentaries, and I did a fair number of documentaries, some of them prize-winning, and I loved that kind of work. But if you wanted advancement, I suppose, you applied for management positions. But I did move around a lot in RTÉ and of that I am proud. I was one of the first people to move, for example, from the programmes area into the news area. And there was a very big division between the two in RTÉ at the time and I managed to straddle both and I managed, I hope, to introduce elements from programming into news to . . .

RG: . . . up the production levels.

JM: Yes, production levels, design, performance, training and various things like that, and of course allied with introducing new

technology which was developing all the time and which consequently has had a huge effect on news and current affairs and indeed programming in general.

RG: The whole canvas of broadcasting has changed throughout
Europe and one thing that we've seen is it's been a bit slower in
Ireland. Certainly we saw it in Europe and then subsequently
from 1979 under de-regulation in the UK with Thatcher, which
marked the advent of the independent production sector. Do you
see that as an improvement or as a hindrance or how do you view
it in terms of farming out programmes to outside production
companies?

JM: Well I do think, perhaps, it leads to more diversity, less
complacency, more innovation, and has contributed some very
good programmes to the schedule, for example looking the other
evening at a profile of John McGahern which was very beautifully
done. Then, of course, other things are not so good but that's the
way it is. I do regret that the pendulum has almost swung too far
in that direction and I would like to see public broadcasters re-
maining producers of programmes. Now that is changing very,
very rapidly and you know, the Channel Four model, where
everything is farmed out, to my mind it was good to keep both in
that that creates its own dynamism.

RG: Finally, what are you doing yourself these days since you
gave up working in RTÉ? You retired there, what, two years ago,
three, is it?

JM: Well it's four years now. I'm doing bits and pieces. I
should be writing more than I am. I've been very much involved
of course in the Magill Summer School which this year celebrates
its 25th anniversary. We've been going for 25 years, an incredible
thought, and of course publishing the books out of that. This year
we published what I consider to be a very good book on political

choice and democratic freedom in Ireland, now available in book-shops may I add!

RG: It has a very heavy line-up of politicians and commentators of one sort or another.

RG: Yes, we've had some excellent contributions, about 40 of them and very honest contributions, worthwhile contributions. So that has taken me a fair bit of time. I still have the old bug of broadcasting and I'm gradually getting back into making a few programmes. I'm involved at the moment in a documentary on the great Irish painter, Louis le Brocquy and I now need to get on with that and get it finished. And I'm hoping to do a few other things.

RG: So you're back as an independent producer then, presumably, or are you freelance in-house?

JM: Well, I'm a kind of hybrid between the two, I suppose. But the important thing is that I keep my hand in there, because I did enjoy broadcasting and I worked hard at it, of course, and I gave it a lot but I think I got a lot from it as well, so I'd like to continue it in some shape or form.

$\mathcal{K}$evin $\mathcal{R}$after

*O*n graduating in Economics from Trinity College, Dublin, Kevin
Rafter worked as an economist with the Dublin Chamber of Commerce and the Fitzpatrick Consultancy whilst moonlighting for Anna
Livia radio. After a year as an economist, Kevin applied for a journalist's
post in RTÉ, got the job and has since worked for some of the most influential media outlets Ireland has seen, from Magill *to the* Sunday Times
and with the state broadcaster at two separate periods of time, for both
radio and television. Now he's back with the Sunday Tribune *as deputy
editor. Despite his busy journalistic schedule, he has managed to pen a
biography of Martin Mansergh and is currently completing a book on
the history of Sinn Féin.*

RG: You studied in both UCD and Trinity. What were your
subjects?

KR: In Trinity it was undergraduate and postgraduate. I studied economics, as a student, and then when I was working in RTÉ in 1996, 1997, I did an MA in politics, part-time, in UCD.

RG: So politics has driven you for quite some time?

KR: Yes, the economics I did in Trinity was public policy which obviously crossed into the political area and then when I went into journalism, my first job was in RTÉ and I ended up presenting the *This Week* programme, which is a current affairs driven programme. I was working on a weekend programme — I'd a few days off in the early part of the week — and I thought it would be good to use my time. I wanted to know more about how the political system worked in an academic sense, so I signed up for the MA in my madness.

RG: Not mad at all, I would have thought, very beneficial. So what persuaded you to get into journalism? Was it the interest in economics or was it the interest in politics or a combination of both, because a lot of people interviewed in this slot seem to have just drifted into journalism?

KR: I suppose I'd be similar to that in a sense. I was recalling this the other night, what actually made me aspire towards a job in journalism. In transition year at school, I did my work placement — I went to secondary school in Limerick, although my parents are now back in Waterford, which is home I suppose — in the *Limerick Post* newspaper, which was a freebie weekly paper driven by ads. But it had an editorial content as well. I spent a week there and I suppose that's when I got the bug. I can recall at school that they brought in people from different walks of life to do interviews with the Leaving Cert students. I put down that I wanted to be a journalist. Jimmy Wolf, who worked for the *Limerick Leader* and was a veteran and famous correspondent in the mid-west, did the interview with me and he asked me lots of questions about politics and current affairs and he had to rate them. He wrote, "Kevin has an aptitude that would absolutely suit him for a job in journalism." So I suppose it came from there but I actually didn't go on and study journalism, I went on to study economics. But when I was in Trinity, I was involved in *Trinity News* and other publications and my first job was as an economist when I came out of Trinity.

RG: With whom or what?

KR: I worked with the Dublin Chamber of Commerce and with the Fitzpatrick consultancy here in town. Even though I had an interest in journalism when I was in college and a lot of what I did was in relation to the publications committee, economics was what I saw myself doing and certainly that's what I started off doing.

RG: So how long were you there and when did you break into journalism?

KR: I left Trinity and I spent about a year working in economic research. But at the same time one evening a week, I worked with Anna Livia Radio, the local community radio station, helping out on the books programme. It was literally helping out, making the coffee for guests and prompting a few questions. Then they were stuck for a presenter for an arts programme for the summer run and I presented that. Even though it was a hobby, it gave me a taste for being in a radio studio. So I was working at the day job, I was doing this on a Wednesday evening and then RTÉ advertised for journalists.

RG: So that was your big breakthrough was it?

KR: I saw the ad and I thought, "I haven't a hope", but if I can get in there and convince them, if they see that I'm really keen for this, then maybe! So I did up the application and sent it in. At the time RTÉ had a trawl for entry-level journalists and luckily I got the interview and on the interview panel were Joe Mulholland, Miriam O'Callaghan from *Prime Time* and Michael Good, who's now head of radio news in RTÉ. I obviously did enough to convince them that I was worth a second look because, at that time, they brought those who came through the interview process to an assessment weekend. It was the weekend of the 1994 World Cup. I know Ireland was playing a match on the Saturday night. We went in on the Friday night. We did a full day Saturday and most of Sunday, compiling radio packages and television packages. There was a collection of people there from the Irish media, people like Paschal Sheehy, John Ryan who went on to do *VIP* magazine and me, who was the non-journalist. For some reason I did enough that weekend to convince them I was worth a try. I remember Joe Mulholland ringing me afterwards and basically redoing the interview with him. At the end he said, "Do you think you can hack it?" So I said, "Well, I think so", and he said, "There'll be a contract in the post tomorrow." So I started in 1995.

RG: And how long were you there that time, because you left RTÉ after how long?

KR: I was in RTÉ for a few years when Geraldine Kennedy offered me a job in *The Irish Times* on the political staff.

RG: You left quite quickly after a year or so?

KR: Just about a year and then I worked with *The Sunday Times* for a short period as political correspondent of their Irish edition. Then the opportunity came up to edit *Magill* magazine. I'd probably still be with *The Sunday Times* in many ways only *Magill*, as everybody in the Irish media knows, has a certain attraction.

RG: It seems to be a great schooling ground for a lot of editors, particularly in its previous life.

KR: I wasn't there that long, just seven months. It was a trying time, but it was an education. Vincent Browne wasn't involved in the magazine at the time, he had sold it to Mike Hogan. But Vincent actually convinced me that it was worth taking the job and I remember saying to my wife Orla, "We don't have kids, if it goes belly up and it doesn't go right, sure I can always go off and do something else." So I lasted about seven months. We did seven issues. It was trying. Mike Hogan probably wasn't, perhaps, the most appropriate man to own *Magill* magazine or to be a magazine proprietor. So that summer I decided I'd had enough and we parted.

RG: But all the while, over the years in journalism, your main fixation has been politics. Would you call yourself a political junkie?

KR: Yes, I would and I don't make any apologies for that. I would consider myself as a political journalist even though the job I do at the moment is public affairs correspondent in the *Tribune*. Most of it is public affairs and I think most of the big stories around cross into the world of politics. I have an academic background in politics and I've written widely about it and lectured about Irish politics, but in terms of journalism a lot of it crosses into the political domain so that is, I suppose, where I have a specialisation. I have an interest and that's probably where I have an advantage maybe, over somebody who really is interested in crime or in business.

RG: Well, as a self-confessed political junkie, do you think the many media outlets in Ireland serve the political junkie well?

KR: I think we get adequate coverage of what goes on in parliament. I think there could perhaps, be more detail in relation to what goes on in the background and in committees. I think some of the politicians may be accurate in saying, "You know, the Dáil will go into recess next week and you'll all say that the Dáil is shut down, whereas there's a month of committee work." Sometimes, maybe, there are aspects of the job the top politicians do that we could keep a closer eye on. But I think — particularly where we've had, in recent years, a weakened opposition — the media has done a good job in keeping an eye on the system. Like the nursing home controversy which has emerged in the last month or so. It was exposed by RTÉ's *Prime Time* and that's an example of journalists keeping an eye on the system which should be monitored and maintained by the political masters. So I think the media and the journalists serve a useful purpose, although the relationship can be fraught.

RG: Do you think journalists in this country are sufficiently investigative in their reporting? A lot of accusations are levelled at certain journalists for reacting to ministers' statements rather than going into any great depth as to what was behind the statement?

KR: I think in any functioning media world you need both reportage, which is effectively providing the facts that the public can make up their own minds about, and opinion, comment and investigation. So I don't think you need one on its own. I think you need a combination of them all in order to get a healthy mix. It's important that when things are reported, they must be reported impartially. Comment and analysis allows for discussion, debate and an examination of those facts.

RG: But the two seem to be merging more and more. The analysis aspect of a story is dealt with before the facts are stated.

KR: Well I think that the media world has certainly changed and competitive pressures are there with the increase in the number of outlets — radio, television and to a lesser extent the print world. The competitive pressures mean that the pressure on journalists to have the story first or to have the better headline or to have the better opening paragraph, is probably higher now than it has ever been before, but you know, while people might complain about that, maybe it's not a bad thing. The cosy consensus and cosy club atmosphere in the gallery in Leinster House has gone. There are brass plates in front of the ten or twelve seats looking down onto the chamber and the brass plates have the name of each of the individual newspapers that would have had a position at that particular time. It has always struck me that it must have been nice and cosy then, whereas I think the competitive pressures now — having multiple outlets — has changed all that, but there's no harm in that either.

RG: You say that journalists should keep a closer eye on politicians. Are we not that good at observing and watching and finding out, do you think?

KR: Well I think it's not even just the politicians, it's the system and the policy formation process. Again, to use the example of the nursing homes scandal or the NIB story or stories in relation to tax evasion, maybe on occasion we've been too attentive to the individual, for example to Bertie and his lifestyle or to John Bruton and his laugh or to Albert Reynolds and particular aspects of his personality. Maybe the attention should be more on the actual system and who is actually making the decisions within officialdom. I think one of the difficulties which came to the fore in Britain during the Hutton Inquiry was that senior policy makers have as much power as senior politicians and sometimes even more, yet we don't tend to follow the civil servants or the officials to the same extent. Maybe that's a weakness and something that will need to be addressed. Particularly given what we've seen in the last couple of years with this plethora of governmental departments that have almost privatised themselves. Aspects like the Prison Service or the Court Service or the Health Service Executive where they're taking over responsibility for policy areas;

that's going to be a big challenge to us as a profession. How do we monitor all of these different agencies who control public policy? In many ways the politicians have divested themselves of the responsibility.

RG: This week, of course, saw the change in the rulings for first-time house buyers but that has largely come, not from Cowen, but from the civil servants. That is a typical example, is it not, of what you're saying?

KR: Yes it is and I think it's also an example of what Dáil Éireann or the Oireachtas badly needs, a far more sophisticated, beefed-up committee system. When these people are brought in and they're questioned or they're asked in front of committees in public session, journalists should be there, taking notes and listening to the answers that are provided. I think that if we had a properly researched and backed-up committee system where scrutiny of the civil servants and the decisions that they're making was much stronger, then, I believe, Irish democracy would be much better.

RG: Do you prefer print, radio or television, given that you've worked in all three media?

KR: They all have their advantages and disadvantages. Television is very satisfying. I worked in recent years on *Prime Time* where you get the big hit and you get time to prepare a story and television obviously has a significant impact. But television is a tabloid medium. It's shallow. Radio provides much more depth, more time.

RG: Interesting what you're saying, that television is tabloid, therefore doesn't commit, perhaps, as much time as it should to politics and current affairs generally. But *Prime Time* does.

KR: *Prime Time* has been excellent in the last number of years in going after a number of significant issues which are obviously of great public concern. RTÉ current affairs do less politics now, I would hazard, than it might have done ten years ago. Less party politics, less politics out of Leinster House, but that's a decision that has been made and it's hard to criticise that, given the ratings that the programme has achieved for the issue-based stories which they've gone after. But I think the issue of depth and satisfaction, whether it's print or broadcast, there are differences between the mediums. In some ways radio is probably the happy medium between them.

RG: And would that be your preference? Because you were on *This Week* every Sunday. Is that your preferred medium rather than the scribbling or the telly?

KR: I'm very much enjoying what we're doing in the *Sunday Tribune* at the moment in terms of trying to re-vamp the paper and provide a quality Sunday read for people and increasing circulation by providing quality news stories. That's a challenge in itself. My attitude has been that I've gone where opportunities have arisen and I think every three to four years it's no harm for people to re-invent themselves and that's one of the glories of the media business, the opportunities one can avail of.

RG: You worked on a variety of stories on *Prime Time*, one of which was Beslan. That must have been a very traumatic experience, was it?

KR: Yes, I suppose, in terms of what I've worked on. The North is the biggest domestic story I've worked on, where people were getting killed on a daily basis. There can be no bigger story. In terms of *Prime Time*, there were a number of things like the exposé on Jim Kennedy, but in terms of just pure, raw emotion, Beslan last September was an experience, a chilling experience, to see such grief up close; to be at a graveyard where there was a queue to bury the bodies of the dead. To see photographs of little girls, twins, their aunts, their grandmother. To go to the morgue and see body parts that had been basically inflamed, was a particularly powerful experience in terms of just the raw emotion. I'm not sure if I'll ever work on a story as big in terms of the impact it had on me personally. It was a part of the world one wouldn't normally go to. It's a part of the world that had almost been bypassed and suddenly the international media arrive into Beslan in the southern part of the Russian Federation, because the Chechen rebels had held the school, the kids, their teachers and some parents in the school building for a number of days; and then the bloody end to that siege. We were very fortunate in that when we arrived there we stayed with a local family, which gave us a unique insight into how locals were feeling and the raw emotion was very, very visible.

RG: You say raw emotion, and I wouldn't put you in this bracket at all, but is there a level of insensitivity by the media in situations like that?

KR: I'm not a war correspondent the way some of my former colleagues are, people like Mark Little or Tony Connolly, who's now in Brussels. RTÉ's Foreign Editor, Margaret Ward, would have specialised in this and it's not something I would aspire towards. Yes, I think it's a very thin line, but what was interesting was when we were there, Casper, the man of the house who we stayed with, said, "You go and you tell the world our story." There's a fine line in terms of intruding on people's grief, but they were looking for answers. The fact that the media was there was putting pressure on Putin's government, because I think if we hadn't been there, there would have been a cover-up or there certainly wouldn't have been explanations. There was one scene where locals had gone to the town hall and they were asking for answers as to why this had hap-

happened and the local military commander told them to go away. He said, "Go away and bury your dead and we'll find the answers later"; and I think that if the media hadn't been there, finding the answers would have been forgotten.

RG: You wrote, as I said in the introduction, a well-acclaimed biography of Martin Mansergh. What prompted you to do a biography on him?

KR: Haughey. Martin Mansergh had been Charles Haughey's senior advisor, his closest advisor for many years. I had begun to write a profile piece on him for *Magill* before I left the magazine. The more I got into it, the more I talked to people, the more I realised it was a really good story. This guy comes from, I suppose, a landed background. He went to college in Oxford, went into the Department of Foreign Affairs and was cherry-picked or hand-picked by Charles Haughey to go and work with him. All of that I found intriguing and I wanted to know more.

RG: It made a very good read. But what fascinated me is the fact that he's not your typical, grassroots Fianna Fáil person, now is he, given his ascendancy background?

KR: No, absolutely not, and as I found out as I did the book and interviewed many people, including Charles Haughey, there was great suspicion of Martin Mansergh within the Fianna Fáil parliamentary party when he first went to work with Charlie Haughey in the early eighties, because he wasn't your typical back-slapping, hail-fellow-well-met Fianna Fáiler. This guy came with a doctorate. He came with an Anglo-Irish accent, but he also had core beliefs and values in relation to Northern Ireland and the national question which were very much in tune with Fianna Fáil. So an intriguing subject.

RG: Now you're back with the *Tribune,* just to wrap up on that. How is the *Tribune* going at the moment? Are you enjoying your role there as deputy editor?

KR: Well I'm three months in. Nóirín Hegarty, the new editor, is four months in and there's a plan in place and hopefully by early next year, people will see a changed newspaper. It's going to be slow and incremental as we make changes and as the paper develops. Already there's a stronger product on a Sunday morning. The objective is that it will be a good, strong, news-driven paper, with strong features and informative comment and analysis. That's the challenge; that's what attracted me to moving to the *Tribune.* Another thing is, I've just completed a book, a history of Sinn Féin, and that gave me the desire to get back into the world of print. As I was writing the book, I realised how much I enjoyed the writing process. When Nóirín offered me the job in the *Tribune,* the book was coming to an end and I think it sort of prompted me. But it was the challenge of what she wants to do with the newspaper. People will pick it up on a Sunday morning and know that it is a quality paper with a good read. Also, from my point of view, being part of that editorial process is exciting.

$\mathcal{D}$enis $\mathcal{T}$uohy

F or the past 40 years Denis Tuohy has been one of the best-known faces on television news and current affairs programmes in Ireland and Great Britain. Born in Belfast, he began his distinguished broadcasting career with BBC Northern Ireland before leaving these shores four years later to join what was then the brand new television service BBC2. He has worked on many flagship news and current affairs programmes, not just with the BBC but also with ITV. Programmes such as **24 Hours, Midweek, Tonight, TV Eye** *and* **Panorama,** *on which he interviewed countless political figures, celebrities, the famous and indeed the infamous. At the time of this interview, Denis had just published his autobiography.*

RG: Your memoir, *Wide-Eyed in Medialand: A Broadcasters Journey*, has just been published by the Blackstaff Press. It's a gripping read, I have to say, and throws up a host of characters and world leaders over the past thirty years. But what may surprise your readers, and indeed our listeners, is that your career as a broadcast journalist was almost a second choice career, because you started out as an actor. Can you tell us about that?

DT: Yes, I had done a great deal of acting at Queen's University in Belfast. I was a very enthusiastic actor and I thought that that probably, with luck, would be where I would make my career and I'd also done some professional work while I was still at university. I worked in a repertory theatre in Bangor, County Down, where James Ellis, or Jimmy Ellis, was the producer and I had done pretty well as a university actor. I'd picked up awards here and there and the signs were that I had, perhaps, what it takes.

RG: As you say you were a university actor and you were in Queen's University. What did you study there?

DT: I studied Classics because I was reasonably good at it and I thought I would get by whilst not doing too much work as I wanted to spend a lot of time doing other things like acting and debating and university journalism, things like that which detracted from my academic progress. But with Classics I thought I'd just get by and I did!

RG: So clearly the acting bug had bitten you at that stage?

DT: Well to go back a bit, it had bitten me at school, Clongowes, where we did school plays just like many schools do. The tradition had started whereby one of the pupils actually produced the school play. In my final year I had produced "Twelfth Night" having been in a couple of plays before with other people producing. So I had experience of acting and producing. I'm not talking about the quality of either the performance or the skill of producing, but certainly it had nurtured an interest and enthusiasm. So as soon as I went up to university, I joined the Dramatic Society.

RG: While there, you were part of a cast that went to Stratford-on-Avon. That's getting into the serious league, isn't it?

DT: Yes, we felt very satisfied in being selected because it was a year when the theatre, the Stratford professional theatre, had decided to organise an open air festival by the river, picking three universities from around the British Isles to take part and we were one of the three that they chose. It was a definite honour and it was, for somebody who was interested in professionally going into the job, a wonderful opportunity to meet a lot of very famous people and be seen by them.

RG: And talking of famous people, you worked with Micheál Mac Liammóir and Hilton Edwards in the Gate. What had you done there, what sort of level, was it walk-ons or did you get to a more serious level?

DT: No, well I didn't actually work with Micheál Mac Liammóir, I was coached by him for an Edinburgh Festival series of plays that Trinity College were doing and they invited me down from Belfast to join their group.

RG: You joined DU Players, isn't that right?

DT: I did for that particular tour to Edinburgh.

RG: The famous Players' Theatre in numbers three and four in the Front Square of Trinity College, where I trod the boards many a time and many years ago!

DT: Isn't that a wonderful place?

RG: I think it's gone now. They built a new, purpose-built theatre down by the rugby pitch.

DT: But wasn't it a wonderful place? We were doing a series of Yeats plays including the prologue to one of them, *The Death of Cuchulain*. He's an old man sort of ranting about modern life and modern Ireland. It's not very much to do with the play, the content of the play, at all, but it's there and it was decided that I was going to have to play this part. I had no idea where to start and someone said, "Why don't you go along and see Micheál Mac Liammóir?" Micheál knew Yeats and because this piece was more or less in the persona of Yeats himself, Micheál was the man for some advice. So I go off to meet Micheál in Harcourt Terrace and the coaching consisted of me reading this prologue and he'd sit and listen. And then he got up and he declaimed it. Then I would read it again and then he would declaim it again and tell me I was doing splendidly. At the end of an hour or so I had to leave. I went back and I delivered it at the next rehearsal in Trinity and they said, "We've no idea whether it sounds like Yeats or not but it's a very good take off of Micheál Mac Liammóir."

RG: Nice story. You worked with another colossus of the theatre, radio, stage and indeed film, Orson Welles. When I say worked, I'm probably stretching it a bit. You had a walk-on when he was playing a series of Falstaff extracts from the various Shakespeare plays in which the character appears, isn't that right?

DT: Yes, that's quite right. He was actually doing the bits of Falstaff that occur in various different Shakespeare plays, all put together, and this was in the Opera House in Belfast. I was out of work at the time and I was still hoping that my acting career would take off and they were looking for extras for walk-ons, as you say, for this production. I was paid — this was 1960 — ten pounds for the week as a walk-on. I would have found ten pounds and paid them in order to be on stage, within a few feet of this extraordinary man whose presence was just so overpowering!

RG: Obviously very overpowering, because there's a photograph in your book of him padded out for Falstaff and he looks absolutely huge. Was he a terrifying person to be around? Some of the many biographies and documentaries portray him as an ogre. Maybe I'm totally wrong.

DT: I know enough stories about him from other people — one particular person who once worked with him as his secretary — to know that that side of him certainly did exist. But I have to say that his treatment of us, the rabble, in both senses — rabble as characters and rabble in relation to him in status — was very kind and generous-hearted. What I particularly remember in terms of the difficult side of him was that he was interested in everything on the stage. He wouldn't necessarily interrupt someone's performance, but the next time there was a break, he'd have a comment to make, even though he wasn't the director, about how somebody else was delivering a line. Or about the costume that one of the stewards was wearing at the back. He'd ask whether that was the right sort of costume for the time and would want to talk about it. So everything — and I suppose this is the movie director in him — that was going to be seen or heard mattered to him.

RG: I want to move on to your association with the playwright Sam Thompson. Can you contextualise Sam Thompson because not everyone is going to be familiar with his work? He died what, it must be 25 years ago, I suppose?

DT: Or even further back. Sam was a shipyard worker who took to writing in his thirties and he wasn't really known as a writer until he was nearly 40. He did some radio dramas for BBC Northern Ireland, but his big break came with a play called *Over the Bridge* which deals with sectarianism in a Belfast shipyard and how it deteriorates into violence. It's a kind of black comedy because there's a lot of fun and humour in it as well. Now when this play was written, it was meant to go on in the Group Theatre in Belfast which was a theatre that had an Arts Council subsidy. It was funded in part by public money, in other words, and the board of the theatre decided that the play — and this is 1959 remember — was likely to cause unrest and that these things should not be put on the stage. Those were the days when the lid was kept on the "troubles" in Ireland, by the establishment, and this play could lead to trouble and it was vetoed. The consequence was that the actors and the director who worked in the Group Theatre said, "All right, we quit, but we're going to put this play on somewhere." It was actually put on in what was then called the Empire Music Hall in Belfast, which was a bigger theatre anyway and where it played to packed audiences. It was a wonderful success and one of the wonderful things about it, in terms of people's theatre, was that the trade unions made block bookings and came along with their wives and families to see a play in which they, themselves, were not looking all that wonderful and generous-hearted, but they were fascinated by the subject. It was a local play, about them, and they wanted to see it and it broke all box office records in Belfast. It then moved to Dublin and did very well.

RG: And it was when it moved to the Olympia in Dublin that you applied to BBC Northern Ireland for a job as an announcer whilst you were in that production of *Over the Bridge*. How did that come about?

DT: I didn't apply with any great enthusiasm because I still hoped that I was going to make it as an actor and partly because my mother had seen this advertisement and was a bit concerned that I wasn't working very much. They'd spent a lot on my education and wondered why I couldn't do better than this and I put in for it and was, to my surprise, invited for interview. I say surprised because BBC Northern Ireland had never, at that stage, appointed a Catholic to be an announcer or indeed a producer.

However, I was invited up for an interview while I was in the run of the play and against the odds in terms of its practices — its sectarian practices if you like — I got the job.

RG: And you moved on from that fairly quickly, didn't you, because within two years you were presenting an early evening light news or magazine-type programme?

DT: Yes, I didn't want to be an announcer for all that long when I joined the BBC and I hoped I would find my way into reporting which I did as a local news reporter. I was also chairman of a satire series, which was very new for BBC Northern Ireland in 1964, called *The Sixty Four Group*. It gibed at the activities of extreme orange and extreme green elements in Ulster society — to popular acclaim it has to be said. That was a most enjoyable series.

RG: But as a Catholic in BBC Northern Ireland at that time, did you feel there was a glass ceiling perhaps — in terms of being a Catholic and moving up the ladder, because that was the 1960s as you say.

DT: I don't think so. I think the breakthrough was getting in, but from the moment that they decided to employ me, everything was fine. I had very good relationships, not just with my fellow reporters and producers and so on, but with the hierarchy and even with the Head of Programmes who had been anxious about a Catholic being appointed to the job, and had said so to the Chairman of the Board that appointed me. Even he and I became, I would say, good friends and he was very encouraging in my career.

RG: Within four years, in 1964, you were invited to go to London when BBC2 Television was starting off and in fact you were the first voice and person on it. But the opening night really was the night that wasn't.

DT: Yes, the most disastrous start, I imagine, in the history of television. There was a fire at Battersea Power Station which provided the power for west London and that included the BBC Television Centre and consequently blacked out the whole area. That meant that BBC2, the new channel, could not start that evening. It was absolute shock horror and indeed there were some paranoid senior members of the BBC staff who reckoned this was a sabotage job by ITV, which is somewhat ludicrous to put it mildly. There's never been any evidence of that and one man said to me "and there never will be", which is an indicator of how upset people were.

RG: But you describe in the book that all was going very well and you'd even gone to the BBC bar for a "steadier" as you described it in the book . . .

DT: Just the one!

RG: . . . and then all hell broke loose didn't it?

DT: Absolutely. I came back about twenty minutes before this opening programme was due to start and others hadn't yet arrived back. I was the first to arrive back and I was somewhat mystified to see that all the monitor screens in the studio and in the production gallery were blank. They should have been showing BBC1 and ITV, never mind our studio and while I was thinking it was a bit strange, I wondered if it was some sort of technical check-up which I didn't understand. Then I remember people running along the corridor towards the studio saying, "Oh my God, there's been a fire in Battersea, there's no power, we're blacked out, we can't go on." And we couldn't and we didn't.

RG: But then the following night, you had a second go.

DT: Well we had a second go and we devised this rather ludicrous little joke whereby you would first of all see a darkened studio with a candle burning on a desk and at the appropriate time, when the programme was due to start, I would appear, pick up the candle, blow it out and all the studio lights would come on and that would be the only reference to what had happened the night before, because everybody knew. It had been all over the papers. It was the biggest story of the day and what were we going to say — "Sorry about that fire last night"? So we didn't refer to it at all except by this sideways joke.

RG: You worked with a number of well-known people in the BBC. People such as David Attenborough who, of course, we all associate with his superb wildlife programmes, but back in the early seventies he was controller of programmes in BBC2.

DT: He was controller of BBC2 programmes earlier than that, from 1965, and then he became overall controller of programmes.

RG: Was he, or is he, better suited to making wildlife documentaries than to television administration?

DT: I would say he was well suited to both, possibly because he had this other side to him, this creative compulsion which had to do with natural sciences, making them popular and explaining them and perhaps because it wasn't the be-all and end-all of life to wear a suit and be an executive. But in fact, he was a superb executive. Also it was a channel in which he was allowed, in those days, to express his own range of interests in the programmes that he commissioned. David Attenborough is a kind of renaissance man, a scientist, but also interested in the arts, literature, music, sport. All of these things he cares about and a lot of what BBC2 achieved in those years was a reflection of Attenborough's range of interests and knowledge.

RG: Coming back to your book, Denis, *Wide-Eyed in Medialand*, which is a memoir of your journey as a broadcaster, there is one thing that is intriguing and that is the chapters and various mentions you have of the Manson/Tate/La Bianca murders, particularly something you did in Sunset Strip, a collection of interviews.

DT: We were surprised, we being myself and Anthony Summers, who's just written a book on Frank Sinatra. But before he took to writing books, he was a producer with whom I travelled a lot. Tony and I were on the west coast of America on a trip for a BBC current affairs programme and we wondered if there was anything we could do about the Tate/La Bianca murders. This was at a time, some months after the killings, when Manson and the others, who were subsequently found guilty, were in jail awaiting trial. Somebody tipped us off that the other members of the group, of the cult, had gone back to live in the Old Movie Ranch, as it was called, that they had been living in at the time of the murders. We thought, "Well, somebody would have found them by now if they had"; and to our amazement, there they were. They were somewhat weird and they accepted us, let us come in and do some filming, mainly because we weren't American and because we said we were from Britain. They said, "Do you know the Beatles?" and we said, "Do we know the Beatles! I was talking to Paul only yesterday", and we were accepted for a while, although they decided they didn't like us after a few hours. But they let us film and talk to them.

RG: You also refer to the fact that they felt they had a claim over some of Lennon and McCartney's music.

DT: Yes, they thought that "Helter Skelter", for instance, was an indication of the destruction of the world that was imminent and from which the family would escape, as long as they retreated to a cave in the Mojave Desert, while the final war took place between good and evil. They would then emerge and take over the world and that was all pre-figured in "Helter Skelter" they believed and one or two other songs that the Beatles had recorded.

RG: A person who exerted much influence over this country, be it good or bad, was Margaret Thatcher. How did you get on interviewing her?

DT: Taxing, combative — I note that she, in her memoirs, describes it as the most hostile interview over the 1979 campaign. Hostile is a very interesting choice of word. It springs from the fact that, I think, for Margaret Thatcher and for other politicians too, but to a remarkable degree for Maggie Thatcher, the world is divided between "them and us" and if you are not one of us, you are one of them — and I was one of them. The interviewer's job is rather like a barrister's brief in a situation like that — to challenge the views, which is a practice used by lots of other interviewers before and since . . .

RG: Not one that President Bush welcomes, but anyway . . .

DT: No, not one that President Bush welcomes! But certainly she didn't welcome it! After it was over, when the battle was over if you like, she was sweetness and light in the hospitality room afterwards.

RG: Finally, not so long ago you appeared in *Fair City*, so you're really back to where you started.

DT: Ha, ha, well I was in a special edition of *Fair City*, a freestanding edition and was I thrilled! Somebody that had known me years and years ago, met me at a party when I was actually trying to lobby an RTÉ executive with some programme ideas for documentaries — without success — and this other fellow said,

"Why don't you try acting again?" I'd never thought of it. I really hadn't thought of it and he said, "You can act and you've been around cameras long enough so that's not going to bother you." So with his help, I got an agent and the agent in due course got me this part which, I must say, I enjoyed.

*J*ohn *W*aters

F or decades John Waters has had his forthright views published and he has been an opinion former and cultural commentator from the so-called darker days in Ireland to the dawn of the Celtic Tiger. On a weekly basis his opinion columns have enraged, provoked or delighted readers of The Irish Times. *As well as being a columnist he has written a number of books, campaigned on issues close to his heart and is a regular contributor to Newstalk 106.*

RG: First of all, can you tell us about your background: growing up in Roscommon, education and what brought you to the capital and ultimately journalism?

JW: I'm from Castlerea in County Roscommon; that's where I grew up and I went to school there, local schools up to secondary level. Then I went to work with CIÉ, the railway company, and I worked in Claremorris, Westport and Galway. I came to Dublin for a while and did various odd jobs here and there before going back down to Roscommon where my father had a mail car which he drove under contract for the post office and I drove that for a few years. At the same time I started to write about music and do music reviews for *Hot Press* magazine.

RG: So you were based in Roscommon when you started to write for *Hot Press*?

JW: I was. When I started off I did both together, writing and also driving for my father. You couldn't survive on the *Hot Press* income in those days, so I did both. Eventually they invited me to come to Dublin to work for *Hot Press* full-time, which I did about 20 years ago.

RG: And had you intended to write about more than music?

JW: I started off writing about music because when I started off, *Hot Press* was an exclusively music paper. I pushed to make it more political and I initiated the political interviews which they've been running ever since. I remember the first one I did was with Michael D. Higgins back in 1983 and he subsequently started to write a column for *Hot Press*, so the magazine broadened out and I broadened out with it.

RG: Well Michael D. would have been a bit of a local hero, or otherwise maybe?

JW: No, for me he was, very much so. At the time, I suppose, I was a bit of a leftie and I even campaigned for Michael once, in a European election, I think it was. I always had an ambition to write from quite early on and I still have a couple of letters at home from various personnel departments of newspapers which make quite tragic and pathetic reading, as they'd sympathetically say, "You haven't a hope of becoming a journalist without a university degree."

RG: So they weren't just "Dear John" letters, if you'll forgive the pun?

JW: They're sad and as I say, I think I still have one or two of them. I think I have one from Independent Newspapers telling me what to do and it looked insurmountable as a series of obstacles.

RG: Really, and some of them stated you didn't have a hope without a degree? But a lot of them would eschew that because, particularly back then, there were the two camps. One was the people who were anti the fellows and women with degrees in politics or arts coming into newspapers; and the hardliners would have said that the copy boy or girl entry level is the best route.

JW: The copy boy thing had gone out a little bit. There were various ways. You could go in with a degree or you could also go to a journalism college like Rathmines, that was another route which was suggested to me. There was a third route, which was the freelance route, but in general I could see that seemed to be pretty hopeless. Nevertheless I did start to write for *Hot Press* and I started purely on spec. I used to send in the odd review. I'd go to a gig and I'd write a review and I'd sent in quite a few before I got one published. Then it would be a long period again, so I just kept trying.

RG: So back in the early eighties, when you started, it was far more difficult to get into the media than it is now?

JW: Well, it seemed to be. Certainly from down where I was, in Castlerea in County Roscommon, it was extraordinarily difficult. There are things that you don't think about now in the age of mobile phones and e-mail, you know? Just basic communications with Dublin was quite primitive. I mean in order to ring Niall

Stokes, the editor of *Hot Press*, I had to go around the town collect-
ing five-penny pieces for a morning to make a call in a call box. So
it was a different world.

RG: About two years ago you wrote that *Hot Press* had embarrassing datedness in its "obsessions with sex, political correctness
and socialist politics" — three subjects which would indeed have
been very hot for *Hot Press* back then — but how do you feel it's
changed?

JW: Well I feel that the difficulty is that I change all the time
and I feel that unless you register those changes in yourself and in
your work, you become out of touch. There's this sort of notion of
a belief in a false form of consistency. I think a lot of those publications and people who started off back then in the sixties or seventies with a particular agenda have been promoting that agenda
ever since, regardless of the fact that everything's changed and
the wars have all been won. Now we have the mess left by the
wars and they refuse to look at those things and that's certainly
what I would feel about *Hot Press* today. It's still fighting a kind of
phantom enemy which is long dead.

RG: At the moment, of course, you enjoy a fairly lofty position
in *The Irish Times* as a columnist. What levels of responsibility do
you have to take on board, given your status as an opinion former?

JW: Well I guess there are quite serious responsibilities in certain contexts. You would certainly be conscious of the responsibility of being factually accurate and all that kind of obvious stuff.
But I think my responsibility — and I'm speaking personally — in
the way I've always seen my job is that because I actually came
from a different place, geographically and also educationally . . .

RG: . . . and culturally . . .

JW: . . . yes and culturally, that that place and those places were not represented in the media. I felt that my responsibility was to represent those things. So I suppose I've become a sort of advocate of unpopular causes, because I look and I listen and I hear things that to my ear are out of joint, out of place, and that there are absent elements. There are parts missing and I try and identify those missing parts and try to articulate them.

RG: You mentioned that when you started off you felt that certain geographical areas of the country were not represented or not properly represented in the media. Have you seen a change in that?

JW: There has been a change, yes, but not necessarily in the national media. I think there is still quite a . . .

RG: . . . are we still Dublin-focused?

JW: Very much, the newspapers are very Dublin-focused, RTÉ is still very Dublin-focused. I think what has changed things is the local radio phenomenon, which has really made a big difference and it's given people a stronger sense of their own voice.

RG: And how do you see that — because presumably you stay in touch with Roscommon — the local radio station has improved things socially, culturally, economically in the hinterlands of this country, as opposed to the local newspapers, which have been around since the beginning of the last century?

JW: There's a stronger sense of a "voice" coming on radio, more so than in newspapers. There's a sense that a newspaper is the property of its proprietor and its controllers. With broadcast media, particularly radio, there's a much stronger sense that it belongs to the people because you hear people's voices on it.

RG: Is that because of immediate interaction?

JW: Yes it is; with phone-ins there's a sense of the immediacy of the response that you get on radio. There's a sense of people talking to each other and that has given great confidence to people in various parts of the country. They have a voice and even though it's not a national voice, it's sufficiently loud in their own area and they can get across their point of view to their local representatives, for example. Previously there was a tendency that the local representative would be listening to the national voices and maybe making up his or her mind on the basis of that a great deal of the time. It has changed subtly and I think has fed people their own power and their own sense of belonging to a larger pattern.

RG: And that was denied them in the local newspapers you feel? You said it was more proprietary.

JW: Yes, it was quite formulaic and convention-ridden really. The format of local newspapers was very rigid and old-fashioned. It's changing now. It's interesting and maybe local radio has had an influence on that as well, it has livened up the newspapers. There was a time when it was just local notes and court reports and social events. There was very little dialogue or discussion or analysis or participatory stuff.

RG: And letter pages were thin, to say the least.

JW: Yes and there was no sense of how you might engage in a discussion or debate about your own area and that really had a massive effect. I mean, in my own town of Castlerea, I wrote in my book *Jiving at the Crossroads* 15 years ago about the appalling effects of the local town trust, as it was called. It was a kind of a local council, not quite a council because there was no democratic element to it; the secrecy of it, the fact that they weren't telling people how they were spending their money. That's beginning to be challenged. The local councillor there, Luke Flanagan, who's been elected to the council, is fighting a very vigorous and successful campaign to flush out the secrets of the trust. So that's an example in my town but that would have been quite a stagnant pool, politically and democratically.

RG: So you say that the people get a better voice on the radio than, perhaps, in the local newspapers. You're a columnist and as such your views get aired but the people who disagree aren't afforded the same latitude from which to put forward their point of view. For example, on one of your own issues, single mothers may feel diminished by your fathers' rights campaign. Would that be an issue you would consider or do you just forge ahead with your own viewpoint?

JW: Well I don't, you see. I don't think that single mothers are in any way diminished by my fathers' rights campaign. That's a completely spurious view that's been put forward by people who don't want to deal with the fathers' rights issue. The vested interests on this issue, for a long time, have been trying to present this as irreconcilable and intractable difficulties between fathers and mothers about children, about some kind of pool of rights which are held in common, but not quite divided properly.

RG: But not written anywhere, necessarily, so it is a conditioning.

JW: But it isn't about that. This is about whether or not fathers should have any rights at all — that's what it's about. It isn't about mothers' rights. Nobody that I have ever met or ever heard or spoken to has ever questioned one iota of the right of mothers to have their rights as mothers. So it's not about mothers' rights. That's a completely spurious argument that's put forward. This is about whether fathers should be allowed to stick their noses across the boundary of their children's lives, that's what it's about. So there is no issue about mothers having a right of reply. There's no issue of mothers feeling genuinely or rightly affronted by what I say. There's a lot of disingenuous affront by people who want to bury this argument and want to prevent this thing being discussed at all.

RG: You say they want to bury it, but what I was referring to there is that a columnist, some would say, should argue "on the one hand this on the other hand that". But you are renowned and have made your reputation from putting forward a singularity of view?

JW: But I think that's what a columnist is. Other people can have their own views. An opinion column isn't really an opinion column either, you know. What I do is tune into society, to life in Ireland and in the world, and seek to articulate those things which come to me, whether they're through other people's voices or through my own experience and I bring to that my whole life experience. I don't intellectually, in an abstract way, set down a series of arguments. I bring the voice of my own life, out of my own life and out of my own experience, and put it into print. I don't have a responsibility to put two points of view or to balance my points of view. If other people disagree with me they have their right to respond. They have the letters page. I've been attacked for years by other columnists on all kinds of issues. Groups, lobby groups, vested interests who don't always reveal their own interest. And also, what I say is such a marginal viewpoint which nobody else, by and large, puts across and I'm talking now about fathers' rights or issues like that, or male suicide, for example, an issue which has been completely neglected for 15 years

RG: Patterns are emerging and it seems to be increasing.

JW: They are and only now are we beginning to have an honest reporting of the facts in relation to suicide and that it's now beginning to be stated reasonably regularly that the problem is young males. It took 15 years to get to that point and I was attacked time and again by psychiatrists, by women's groups, by all kinds of people, priests even, trying to stop this discussion for whatever reason.

RG: But has your campaigning journalism, which is perhaps a better way to express it, had any effects? Is there progress in your battle for fathers' rights, do you think?

JW: I would never claim any success for myself because I would be modest about the ability of columnists to effect direct change. I don't think that's the way it works.

RG: It can bring about change, surely, by raising the issues, which you've done.

JW: You can certainly motivate people and you can have an effect, you can be part of a discussion. I think there have been changes, in the sense of society becoming more aware. But there certainly is not change in the system. You have a system in relation to the family law courts which, if it existed in any other context or in any other society and we became aware of it, would have people marching. Amnesty International would be marching up and down the streets on a daily basis and they have nothing to say at all about this kind of thing because it happens right under our noses, where the most fundamental human rights of people are abused by people who have no accountability, no transparency, no ability to deal with the issues that they're dealing with because they're not trained and they know nothing about it. I'm talking now about judges. It is the most appalling brutality done in your name and my name in this society and it is only with the greatest difficulty over the past decade that I've been able to articulate a tiny fraction of what's going on.

RG: You're talking about visitation rights and access, particularly in relation to the judiciary, what they mete out and what they would see as a balanced solution.

JW: Judges, particularly District Court judges, brutalise fathers. I have a half dozen or more fathers writing to me every week with stories that really are beyond belief. You would think that in a so-called modern society, human beings could behave in this way towards one another; that a judge could sit on the bench and tell a man in relation to his children that he shall only see them once a month or that he shall go to jail if he does this or that — in relation to his *children*! I mean it is quite staggering; but what is even more staggering is the corruption of the media which has allowed this to go on, because I brought it to the attention of the media here and yet there's no coverage of it. There's no interest in covering it. And the only interest that I've detected in relation to the media is an attempt, over the last decade, to shut me up. So fundamentally what I believe that does is it questions — in my mind anyway and I think it should pose the question in the minds of other people — the very integrity of the media to investigate anything or to have any ethical view of power and how it behaves. Because if journalists are not prepared to investigate and to deal with these corruptions, right under their noses, how in the hell can they be trusted to deal with anything else?

RG: OK, I want to move on. In relation to the recent controversy regarding Kevin Myers and the "mother of bastards" article, you took exception to his treatment by *Irish Times* editorial staff. Are you still of the same opinion on that?

JW: I came out against the paper on that issue and yes I am of the same view. I had great sympathy towards Kevin and I also have great admiration for Kevin as a journalist. I think he's a fabulous journalist.

RG: As do I . . .

JW: He made a mistake but the problem was that he wasn't protected editorially and the situation developed and wasn't dealt with in time. So yes, I do have that view still. But it's in the past now. It's dealt with and it's finished with and Kevin Myers is still a brilliant journalist.

RG: Has he changed, do you think?

JW: I hope not. We all have limits to what we can say and things we want to say and boundaries that we want to push out and sometimes we push over. I do it, we all do it, and that's what the editing process is about.

RG: Is the editing process letting Kevin Myers down, or maybe yourself down, when it comes to it?

JW: Well, we're all frail and human . . .

RG: And we all have emotions and we need to express them.

JW: Yes, and that slipped through for all kinds of reasons and it shouldn't have. I mean there's no question that it can be justified in any way, shape or form. But these things happen. I think it's also very important that we do need to know how far we can go because we need to go that far and that's not an exact science.

RG: When you're talking about any issue, be it yours or the issue that Kevin took up at that stage, does it require, sometimes, a shock tactic, apart from a strong opinion, from a journalist? If there is no reaction, then only shock value is going to get that reaction.

JW: I do agree with that and that's why it becomes dangerous because if you are doing what I do or what Kevin does, sometimes your judgement can be a little off and, yes, it does. I fully believe that change is never achieved by reasonableness. It's achieved by unreasonableness . . .

RG: . . . by confrontation?

JW: Yes. You could actually argue that some of the things that I've written over the years were over the top and people will argue that. But the question is, would they have attracted so much notice and would people be talking about the fathers' rights issue in Ireland, would they be now talking about suicide, if people were not prepared to actually say quite strong things? It's very interesting — people always demand that you be moderate in your response and when they do, you find that behind that demand is an opposition to your argument. It is very rarely a genuine issue.

RG: John, finally, you had your own troubles with the editor of *The Irish Times* in relation to comments you made regarding the pension and pay-off to former editor Conor Brady. Can you talk us through that, what happened and how things are now between yourself and the editor?

JW: Well it was broader than simply Conor Brady. It was about an entire situation in which . . .

RG: In relation to the Trust . . .

JW: . . . the Trust and payments to directors in the context of huge redundancies having been put through the previous year. So because there was a sense within the paper that this was wrong and should be written about. Here we were, writing about everybody else's foibles and we were not prepared to write about our own. I took up the challenge. I was challenged pretty robustly by a colleague and I said, "Well, OK, you have a point, I will write about it", and the piece was passed for publication and was subsequently withdrawn. Then the thing went public and certain things were said. Offence was taken at something I said and that's fair enough, but things have resolved themselves now. I think, and I don't want to be political about this or to sound like a politician, but you can actually have, I believe, robust differences of opinion and you should be able to survive them, and I feel that's all in the past in a certain sense.

RG: And above all, you should be allowed to express them.

JW: Well you should, yes, and I greatly believe that there is no damage to be done by people expressing their views in general. There are limits, as I say and, well, we found, I think, in the Kevin Myers thing, that a limit was breached there. Clearly there are certain things which should not be said or should not be countenanced or which should not be encouraged. It's a very difficult argument because you don't want to feed people who will actually close down any discussion. There was an attempt, for example, to close down Kevin Myers on the general issue of unmarried mothers and so on. That was an improper use of that episode in the interests of censorship and I think that's a different issue. It's quite a complex argument but it's one that's ongoing.

From Left: **Media Matters** *producer, Paddy McDonnell,*
Roger Greene, programme contributor Bryan Regan